Mickey Mantle's

Mickey Mantle's

BEHIND THE SCENES IN AMERICA'S MOST FAMOUS SPORTS BAR

WILLIAM LIEDERMAN

THE LYONS PRESS
Guilford, Connecticut
An imprint of The Globe Pequot Press

To buy books in quantity for corporate use
or incentives, call **(800) 962–0973**
or e-mail **premiums@GlobePequot.com.**

The Lyons Press is an imprint of The Globe Pequot Press.

10 9 8 7 6 5 4 3 2 1

Printed in the United States of America

ISBN: 978-1-59228-843-4

Library of Congress Cataloging-in-Publication data is available on file.

To Chloe, my outstanding editor and wonderful daughter.

After the first embellishment, you never exaggerate.

—Mickey Mantle

CONTENTS

FOREWORD

Two things happened the year I was in second grade: my father opened Mickey Mantle's, and I fell victim to my very first crush. His name was Matthew, and I knew little about him except that, (a) he was a Yankees fan (but who wasn't?), and (b) he had a very, very large head. During snack time and recess, I always used to steal little glances in his direction and wonder what was going on in that great big cranial dome of his. Whatever it was, it had nothing to do with me, the little blond in OshKosh overalls pining for him from three desks away. He never even looked in my direction.

"Well, what the hell's the matter with that kid?" my doting father wanted to know. "Doesn't he know that you're the sweetest, smartest, and most beautiful girl in the whole second grade?"

"No," I whimpered, head in hand. "That's the problem: I like him and he doesn't like me."

"Well," my father reasoned, "what does he like? What are his interests? If you like a boy in your class, you should go over and talk to him, find out what you two have in common."

The next morning, I swapped the overalls for my best dress and a pair of patent-leather Mary-Janes. Then I snuck some of my mom's lip gloss and headed for school, single-minded in my focus on the task at hand. Stuffing my coat and backpack into my cubby, I sauntered on over to the boy with the big head before I could talk myself out of it. He was standing alone in a beam of morning light coming through the classroom windows, sorting through a stack of three-by-four-inch cards.

"Hi," I offered, leaning seductively against the desk nearest my crush. "What are you doing?"

"Baseball cards," he mumbled, without moving his eyes from the wad of cardboard in his chubby, grubby hands.

"Cool," I replied. "I have a baseball card, too."

"Wow," he snorted, rolling his eyes, "one whole baseball card. Can I be you?"

"Well . . . it's a really good one," I countered, letting his dig roll off my back. "It's a Hank Aaron."

And with that, I had caught his attention. My heart soared as his eyes met mine for the first time in the conversation. (At four-foot-six, he was the only boy in the class who surpassed me in height, and it was highly romantic.)

"Hank Aaron?" he cried. "You mean an original?"

"Yeah, it's an original," I assured him. "My daddy gave it to me."

"You must have a really cool dad," he murmured, eyes wide with envy. "Is Hank Aaron your favorite ballplayer of all time?"

"Yes," I said, although I didn't really have a favorite. "Who's yours?"

"Mickey Mantle," he declared, without missing a beat.

"So did you talk to him?" my father asked me that evening at dinnertime.

"Yeah," was my uninspired reply.

"And do you think he likes you?"

"No," I said. "He likes someone else."

"And who's that?" my father asked.

"Mickey Mantle."

This pronouncement amused my father to no end, and as he sat there laughing at my expense the way adults so often did, I wished someone would let me in on the joke. As it turned out, it wouldn't be long until someone did.

Several weeks later, my father told me that he was starting a new business, a restaurant called Mickey Mantle's.

"Like the baseball guy?" I asked him.

"Like the baseball guy," he affirmed. "In fact, you'll get to meet the baseball guy next week when he comes into town. The baseball guy is going to be Daddy's new business partner."

This news, of course, went straight back to school with me the next morning, garnering not only Matthew's attention, but that of every other boy in the class to boot. In the few seconds it took me to rattle off the good word, I became the most popular girl in my class. Everyone wanted to sit by me at story time and lunch. Everyone wanted to be my "buddy" for our upcoming field trip to the Museum of Natural History. When I was the snack monitor two days later, and the teacher asked who would like to help me with the job, hands shot up around the room like fireworks on the Fourth of July. It was as if some of Mickey's star dust had rubbed off on me, and everyone hovered close by, hoping to glean some remnant of the majestic fallout.

I was jazzed. My plan was working better than I ever could have imagined, and before long, it was time to raise the stakes. The next week during recess, I let slip to my newfound entourage that there would be a great, big party at Mantle's to celebrate the opening, casually mentioning that tons of stars were going to be there.

"Stars like who?" Matthew wanted to know.

"Stars like Reggie Jackson," I bragged, digging into my memory for the names I had heard my father throw around on the ever-increasing number of business calls that came through our home. "Stars like Don Johnson and George Michael and Ed Koch!" (What can I say? . . . It was the eighties.)

"And don't forget Mickey Mantle," Matthew reminded us, nudging me in the ribs with a freckled elbow. "Mickey Mantle's gonna be there, too, right Chloe?" I loved him so much I thought my heart would sprout wings and fly right out of my mouth.

"Sure he'll be there," I boasted, jutting my chin out ever so slightly. "He'll be there and I'll get you his autograph, if you want it."

The entire playground fell silent for the moment that followed, and I knew I'd be Matt's girl forever. Or at least until Christmas break. Excellent.

"So what's new with big head?" my father asked me later that day.

"Not much," I mused, twirling a golden curl around my finger. "We're going out."

"What? Going where?" he wanted to know.

"Daddy," I sighed, "we're not actually going anywhere. We're just 'going out.' You know, like boyfriend-girlfriend."

"Oh. Swell."

"So I have to get him Mickey's autograph at the big party."

"Is that what he told you?"

"No, that's what I told him."

"Oh, honey," my father sighed, turning me to face him, "don't be promising autographs out to the kids at school. It's a bad idea. What happens if you can't make good on your promise?"

"I didn't promise."

"Promise?"

"Promise."

"Okay," he agreed, ruffling the hair atop my head. "Now go put your shoes on because Grandma will be here any minute. She's taking you to Bloomingdale's to get a new dress for opening night."

Opening Night was well worthy of capital letters. My father unveiled his long-awaited project to a chorus of Dom Perignon corks popping from their long-necked bottles. I remember looking at my father in his tuxedo and thinking, That's my dad. As children, we learn to be proud of ourselves when we learn to read or ride a bike, but this was the first time I could remember feeling truly proud of another person's accomplishments.

For my part, I stepped on Don Johnson's foot, got a live radio interview with Spencer Ross on WFAN, snuck my first-ever glass of champagne, got lost in the crowd (literally), and wound up on Yankee manager Billy Martin's lap as he patted my head and Mickey tried to soothe me with murmurs of, "Don't crah, little darlin' . . . Don't crah . . ."

I also got Mickey Mantle's autograph for my boyfriend. I remember watching Mickey's massive hands, like meat hooks, as he scrawled it across a brand new baseball and personalized it, "To Matthew."

All in all, the night was an outrageous success, and I would ascribe the very same pedigree to the restaurant itself, as it was, and as I will always remember it: my dad's place.

Chloe Liederman

1

WATCHING THE CLOCK

I NEVER LIKED SCHOOL. I was a compulsive clock-watcher. Of course, the more you watch the clock, the slower it ticks. My clearest memories of academia include willing the minute hands of various classroom wall clocks to make their pokey circuits that much faster, and the unbearable restlessness I felt in my wrap-around desk chair.

My clock-watching began at the Little Brook Elementary School in Princeton, New Jersey, and traveled northeast with me to Great Neck South in Great Neck, Long Island, when my parents moved the family there in 1967. I was a gangly junior at South when, about three weeks into the fall term, I wandered into Mr. Stern's Algebra II class late. There I slouched in the doorway, complete with love beads, Indian moccasins, and an oversize belt buckle shaped like a peace sign.

"Mr. Liederman," Stern greeted me, "so kind of you to join us."

"No problem," I told him, giving my shaggy, black hair a righteous toss.

"You're ten minutes late," he observed. "What's your excuse?"

"Algebra is irrelevant to my life," I murmured, as my classmates watched in slack-jawed stupor.

"Excuse me?"

"I said algebra is irrelevant to my life."

Mr. Stern slammed down his eraser, sending wisps of chalky dust into the air like gun smoke.

"If algebra is irrelevant to your life," he announced, "then you are irrelevant to this classroom. Get out."

Of course, there were certain things I liked about school: flirting with girls, free periods, lunch, and gym, to name a few. I'd recently gone from being the class jock/jerk in Princeton to the school hippie in Great Neck. The previous year, I'd won the New Jersey State high school tennis championship tournament, but I didn't want to ruin my new image, so I replaced conventional team sports like soccer, basketball, and baseball with less traditional group activities, such as smoking grass in the woods beyond the playing field and plotting to occupy the school.

By the time senior year rolled around, I was at an age where I thought I knew pretty much everything there was to know about life. So at seventeen, I channeled my nuclear energy into organizing Great Neck South's first ever "Free School" curriculum. Free School was a forum for alternative learning. Subject matter ranged from black power to women's studies to sexual politics and the like. Students actually attended Free School classes during their free periods in order to counteract the numbing effects of irrelevant topics such as Algebra II.

I also headed a huge fund drive for the starving children of Biafra and got Dave Van Ronk to give a benefit concert. I joined a radical studies reading group. In the political tumult of 1969, I helped to found Great Neck South's chapter of SDS, Students for a

Democratic Society. And through it all, I somehow maintained a B+ average. By the middle of my senior year, I'd completed all credits required for graduation except senior English and Social Studies. I wanted my diploma, but I knew it was time for me to bust out of high school.

My father was a professor of psychology at SUNY College at Old Westbury. The university offered an accredited, semester-long Spanish immersion program in Cuernavaca, Mexico, for high school students with good marks in English. Not only would I graduate on time, but I would learn to speak Spanish and earn college credits as well. I'd also return an international man of mystery, and the chicks would dig it. It seemed to me like a real win-win situation.

Since I was only one English class and one history class short of graduation, one of my teachers turned me onto the University of Nebraska Extension School where I could take these two classes through the mail in Cuernavaca and still finish high school on time. The mail-in classes were a tit job, but the opposite was true of Spanish class, where nobody knew *anything*. Four hours a day, Señor Gomez, myself, and three other students would engage in grueling, round-the-table drills. But unlike Algebra II, I knew that Spanish would come in handy. By the time I left Mexico at the end of spring semester, I was pretty fluent in Español. I've since lost a lot of it, but I can still prattle away with the best of 'em in my flattened, gringo staccato. It may be a bit awkward, but it gets the job done.

My accent is sketchy, but my comprehension is pretty sharp. I understand nearly everything I hear in Spanish—a major advantage in the restaurant business. I've tried to hide this ability from my employees over the years, in order to be a fly on the kitchen wall.

A year later, I enrolled in Sarah Lawrence College in Bronxville, New York, as part of the school's first-ever coed freshman class. It had long been a private women's college, but I was about to cross the sexual picket line. In the fall of 1971, I was one of only six intrepid men to infiltrate the system. The administration stuck us half-dozen brave pioneers into a suite in the basement of a women's dormitory and waited to see what would happen.

A large portion of the student body was of the lesbian persuasion—and there was no breaking through that force field. The rest, however, stopped busing to Yale, Princeton, and Harvard for mixers and started looking in their own backyard. They pounced on the six of us like a pack of hungry she-wolves.

This may sound like all that and a bag of chips to any red-blooded American man, but it turned out to be hell on earth. The social pressure became so enormous that I took myself out of the loop and started seeing Rosemary, a beautiful Latina who was studying with my father at SUNY–Old Westbury.

My two fondest memories of Sarah Lawrence are the following.

1. Spanish literature: Mexico had made me good enough to fake my way through class discussions. However, my reading comprehension left something to be desired, so I bought the Cliffs Notes to *One Hundred Years of Solitude* and spun the chapter summaries into witty and deeply insightful Spanish classroom banter about life in Gabriel Garcia Marquez's finely drawn literary landscape. The professor took me for a cunning linguist. Little did she know I'd been hangin' with Cliff. I took home an A–. The handwritten evaluation read as follows: "Bill has outstanding reading comprehension in the Spanish language. His comments on *One Hundred Years* were consistently thoughtful, and demonstrated full command of the material. His conversation

skills, however, leave a lot to be desired. His accent has failed to develop, and his rapid-fire delivery jars the listener. If Bill should choose to continue in this field, I suggest he take a remedial course in Spanish conversation." In retrospect, I think my experience in New York City restaurants has more than fulfilled that requirement.

2. Basketball: Sarah Lawrence maintained an association with Bronx Community College, a few clicks down the Deegan Expressway. I outgrew my anti-jock sentiments and pieced together an intercollegiate Division III college basketball team. I stacked the roster with nine Afro-clad soul brothers from BCC who were taking some classes at Purchase and therefore qualified for the team. Then I called every athletic director in the area, from Concordia to Mercy College to Westchester Community, and rounded up a twenty-game schedule. I beat a few dollars out of the administration for uniforms, refs, and equipment. I hired a former Division I hoopster from Canisius as our coach, and suddenly, before anyone could think of a good reason to stop us, Sarah Lawrence had a men's basketball team.

The last game of the season was against Old Westbury, the very same school where my father, brother, and girlfriend were hanging their hats. I was playing on their turf, and I knew their allegiances were mixed. To make matters worse, my girlfriend had recently dumped me for a girlfriend of her own. Her name was Susan, and the sight of her snuggling up to Rosemary on the bleachers renewed my competitive drive. Stakes were high.

All my life, I've had a recurring dream about getting into that one big game and not being able to find my sneakers. I'd always wake awash in a mixture of cold sweat and superlative relief that it wasn't real. (Mickey Mantle later told me of his own recurring dream: he was late for a game and had to squeeze in through the fence posts at the stadium, a task that always proved impossible.) On that day, my nightmare became a reality. I forgot my sneakers and had to borrow a pair three sizes too small from the team manager.

"If you can't remember to pack your sneakers, you don't deserve to play," said the coach. He was eager to teach me a life-lesson, so for most of the game, I rode the pines. I sulked big-time, thinking that if Leroy Washington, our six-foot-six starting center, had forgotten *his* sneakers it wouldn't be an issue. I watched the lead seesaw back and forth as the game came down to the wire. Two of our guys had fouled out and now the coach had no choice but to play me. With less than ten seconds left in the game and Sarah Lawrence trailing by three points, I hit a "jump" shot from deep in the corner. Then, as Old Westbury tried to inbound the ball, I intercepted it and laid it in for two insurance points. My father and brother joined my team on the court for a victory dance and group hug as Rosemary and Susan filed out of the gym with their hands in each other's back pockets.

Ultimately, I couldn't stomach the precious aesthetic at Sarah Lawrence, so I transferred to SUNY–Purchase, where I majored in History with a concentration in American and Medieval Studies. I worked over my academic advisor for a curriculum full of independent study credits, and for the next three years, my class schedule was limited to one clock-watching day a week. During that day, I would endure four straight hours of independent study tutorials. I wrote papers instead of taking tests, with the help of a few "black beauties." Al Gore hadn't invented the Internet, so despite my bug-eyed proofreading, my work was festooned with dozens of flagrant typos.

My season on the Sarah Lawrence team had left me with a major basketball jones, so I went on repeat mode and organized a Division III team for SUNY–Purchase. The artsy-fartsy student body got to vote on the team mascot and color, so the Purchase Panthers wore heliotrope and puce. I wore these colors proudly for three years, during which time I was voted team captain twice. Career highlights include diving headfirst after a loose ball into a row of nuns at Mercy College, and playing against the undefeated Concordia Vikings. I played in front of a posse of Division I scouts, in a game we ended up losing by fifty points. I ended up accumulating Wendell Ladner–type stats: ten points, ten rebounds, and five fouls.

"The Panthers' best player is that kid Liederman," the opposing coach remarked to a scout within my earshot. "He's not a big-time college prospect, but he's got a ton of heart."

No one had ever accused me of having any real talent for the game, so it pretty much made my decade.

My junior year, I carved out an accredited assistant teaching position for myself at the progressive Little Red Schoolhouse in Manhattan's Greenwich Village. Halfway through the spring semester, the teacher had a nervous breakdown. There I was, a twenty-one-year-old undergrad, waiting in the wings. Because the kids loved me and there were only eight weeks left in the school year, Little Red allowed me to teach social studies and current events all by my lonesome. At the end of the semester, I told them I'd graduated, even though I still had a year to go. This made me an obvious candidate for the newly available full-time position. Private schools require teaching degrees, and the administration trusted me too much to bother checking on my SUNY status. I got the job and commuted, for the next year, from my apartment on the Upper West Side, to school and basketball at Purchase, to my seventh-graders in the West Village, and back again. It was one of the most challenging and thrilling times of my life.

As graduation drew near, I reviewed my transcript and realized I was two credits short of the requirement. In a manic panic, I arranged an independent study in weight lifting with the university's athletic director, Irwin August. The plan was simple: Coach August would test my strength in a diagnostic session and draw up a training plan to build my brawn. I would then train independently throughout the semester, and Irwin would assess my progress at the end of the term. At the diagnostic session, I put forth an Oscar-worthy performance of the world's weakest man, lifting far less than I could actually manage. The goal was to double my capacity by semester's end, so I knew I was golden. My social life and full-time teaching position, combined with basketball and academics, left little time to train. In fact, I didn't pump an ounce of iron that term. But the final exam was a breeze as I made a big show of "struggling" with double the original weight, grunting and groaning for dramatic effect.

"I'm authorizing your two credits," Coach August announced at the end of our session. "Congratulations on a job well done, Mr. Schwarzenegger."

Around that time, my brother David, a professional chef who'd done an internship in France at three-star-rated Trois Grois, launched a start-up frozen foods business called Saucier, making sauce bases such as *Glace de Poulet, Glace de Poisson,* and *Bordelaise.* David was having the Howard Johnson's commissary in Queens Village co-pack the product according to his specs. To make authentic sauce bases, bones are simmered for hours in hot water until the stock boils down to a viscous sauce base. The first time HoJo's ran the product they tossed out the reduced stock and shipped him the bones.

David's fine-tuned, French cuisine sensibilities were lost on the vast majority of Americans, and the company went nowhere fast. Together, David and I brainstormed for something more basic, more mainstream, more appealing to our demographic. The answer was simple: chocolate-chunk cookies, fresh out of the oven, made with real chunks of Lindt chocolate. And so it was that David's Cookies came into the world. When David asked me to take a year off from teaching and become president of Saucier Cuisine, Inc., I jumped at the chance.

However, Saucier was only grossing about $25,000 per year, and I needed a Plan A, B, and C. I leafed through The New School for Social Research catalogue in search of a Business 101 course. In so doing, I noticed that the adult education program offered only a couple of cooking courses—and they were buried in the catalogue. There was a large, fully equipped test kitchen in our office on Madison Avenue and 32nd Street. I called the school, asked for a dean, and made the following proposal: put us in your catalogue, and we'll provide the kitchen-classroom, ingredients, and cooking instructors. Their catalogue was going to press in a week, but the dean, Mike Vollen, said that if I could arrange a list of courses and descriptions before deadline, I was in. I don't think he imagined I could do it. But I did, with time to spare, and The New School Culinary Arts Program was born.

It was the 1980s, and the restaurant business was red-hot. It wasn't long before the student body outgrew the one-kitchen classroom. I borrowed a million dollars from Jamie Niven—son of the actor Sir David Niven, who was one of the original investors in Saucier—and used it to build a three-level, four-kitchen facility on 34th Street between Fifth and Sixth avenues. I called it The New York Restaurant School. It was a terrific success, and after a few short years, we won college accreditation from the State of New York. Our course catalogue boasted over one hundred cooking courses from How to Boil Water all the way up through Advanced French Cuisine. Our tag line was: *Make a career out of your love of food.*

Despite our popularity, we weren't exactly raking it in—what with high rents, instructors' salaries, and the expense of food and supplies. I got my first real taste of the restaurant business when, in an attempt to turn a profit, we opened a precious little forty-seat, student-operated bistro appropriately dubbed The Restaurant at The New York Restaurant School and were critically acclaimed by most of New York's most influential food critics.

In our seventh year of operation, I was approached by a man who was interested in buying the school. He was a "flipper" who went around buying and selling vocational schools. The money he offered was enough to pay off my original million-dollar loan and for me to live for about a year without working. To cushion my landing, I asked for a one-year employment contract. He agreed, but he wanted a three-month cancellation clause, "Just in case."

He made it clear that he was buying the school because of *me.*

"You are the school, and the school is you," he kept saying.

Drunk with his compliments, I signed the deal against my lawyer's advice. A week later, the new owner moved me from my original office overlooking 34th Street to a converted coat closet by the front door, next to the elevators. A month later, he asked me if perhaps I'd be more comfortable working from home. It wasn't long before I got a letter terminating my employment altogether. He was exercising his option to get rid of me, effective immediately. Nobody, not even a cooking school director, is indispensable.

After he kicked me to the curb, I tried to buy a minor-league baseball team. But even in the late eighties, average teams were worth millions of dollars, and my pockets weren't nearly deep enough. With time and money dwindling, I searched for a way to combine my knowledge of the restaurant business with my love of sports. Maybe I would open a sports-themed restaurant. I put together a short list of legendary athletes whose names might look impressive on the marquee. My top three choices were Mickey Mantle, Joe Namath, and Muhammad Ali.

I never got around to the latter two, because Mickey expressed interest right away. After scouting more than fifty locations from the Bronx to the Battery, I selected a space on Manhattan's Central Park South and brought Mickey to the site for his approval. As we rolled up I began to feel a little squeamish about the location. It was right on the park, nestled between the St. Moritz and Park Lane hotels, directly across the street from the quaint horse-drawn carriages. Mick had said he wanted a place where he and his friends could feel comfortable; I wondered if Central Park South would be too froufrou for the ruggedly masculine sensibilities of my childhood hero, who was dressed like the Marlboro Man in a black ten-gallon hat and a pair of snakeskin boots.

Looking something like West Texas meets the West Village, Mickey sauntered in through the revolving doors like a cowboy into the local saloon. Except this was no saloon. This was Les Tuileries, a precious French bistro with terrazzo floors and potted palms. As he narrowed his eyes and surveyed the ruins of the fruity former restaurant, I cringed, wishing I'd scattered some sawdust and peanut shells around beforehand. But as it turned out, Mick was thrilled.

"I can't fucking believe it," he crowed. "This place is fucking perfect!"

Mickey explained that during his playing days with the Yankees, he had lived at the St. Moritz for a couple of seasons. Sometimes, on nice days, he and Billy Martin would hike up through Central Park and on to the Bronx in time for a day game. But an even more astonishing coincidence was that Harry's Bar, the St. Moritz's watering hole, once occupied part of the space now intended for Mickey Mantle's. Of course, Mick and his Yankee pals did their main pounding at Harry's back then. In fact, Mickey spent so much of his leisure time there that he and his ballplayer pals actually called the place "Mickey's Place." And now, after all these years, it really would be Mickey's bar after all.

2

DOING THE DEAL

When it was time to talk turkey, doing Mickey's gobbling was one Roy True, Esq., from Dallas, Texas. If you closed your eyes when Roy spoke, you could almost be listening to Dan Rather. When you opened them, you could be looking at a long-lost Mantle brother. Roy had giggling blue eyes and a snow-white mane, coiffed to Jimmy Johnson perfection.

Mr. True was sitting at the 30-yard line of a massive walnut conference table at the Park Avenue law firm of Pryor Cashman Sherman & Flynn. My first question for Roy was how much money Mick would be prepared to invest in our new restaurant.

With a Texas-style stiff upper lip, he said, "Bill, when you've hit 536 career home runs, you don't have to put up *any* of your own money."

I changed gears: "Okay, then what does Mickey want for the use of his name?"

"Just a $40,000 annual fee, plus 7 percent of the equity, being that Mickey wore number 7."

Before I could respond, my longtime lawyer and friend Ron

Shechtman outlined the downside of celebrity involvement in public restaurants, including liability, high failure rates, and the potential black mark upon Mickey's name if the place indeed went bust. He wanted to test Mantle's mettle and make sure he was serious.

"Oh, yes," Roy assured us, "we've considered all the collateral issues and Mickey is quite comfortable with this arrangement."

The meeting adjourned on a warm and fuzzy note, complete with double handshakes and Texas-style back pounding.

Months later, after final drafts had been minted, leases inked and signed, and an $800,000 construction loan obtained, Mickey Mantle still hadn't signed the contract. For three agonizing weeks, there was no response to our letters and phone calls.

With hope dwindling, True finally called.

"Mickey's been thinking this over," he began, "and he's not entirely comfortable with the arrangement after all. What with the risk of liabilities and . . ."

"How much?" I interjected.

True paused, and then pounced: "He's decided that he'd be more comfortable if his annual fee were to be doubled."

The country bumpkin had hung this city slicker out to dry. I had no choice but to say, "I do."

The next day, FedEx made its appointed rounds, and I received my first Mickey Mantle autograph—his signature on a long-term contract. It was the largest contract he had ever signed, including the six-figure deal for his final season with the Yankees.

Over the next two decades, with the exception of a multimillion-dollar Upper Deck deal, the Mantles made more money from the restaurant than from any other business venture.

3

FIGHTING CITY HALL

NEW YORK CITY DOES NOT make it easy to open a restaurant. One might imagine that because of all the additional tax revenue the city derives from the business, they would bend over forwards and backwards to encourage aspiring restaurateurs to flip their first burgers. The truth is quite the opposite.

First, there's the health permit. You can't get one until you're open, but you can't open without one. Then there's the liquor license. In the State of New York, you have to apply for a new one, unlike in New Jersey, where you can buy the existing license from the previous tenants. The process used to take about nine months, unless you knew someone at the N.Y. State Liquor Authority.

Then there's the "open-flame permit," which you need in order to use candles in your dining room or bar area; and the "dumb-waiter permit," without which you cannot operate—you guessed it—the dumbwaiter.

The list goes on. There's the "ice-cream scoop permit," which ensures that the scooping implement remain in a lukewarm bath while idle, lest deadly bacteria accumulate.

There's the "outdoor cafe permit," which took me three years to acquire. The community board directed me to commission a $20,000 traffic survey, all for six small tables at which visiting Euro trashsters can sip their espressos and chain-smoke Capri lights.

Then there's the final insult: the "revolving-door permit," which I flat-out refused to pay. The inspector told me that if I hired his daughter as a waitress, he'd let me slide on the permit. I did, and she was a wonderful long-term employee. The next best deal I can think of is in *Old Yeller,* when Travis trades a woman-cooked meal and a horny toad for that Old Yeller dog.

I'm sure there are many more necessary permits that I've never even heard of. What never ceases to amaze me is that, although you need a permit to do most anything in life, from owning a dog to getting married, you *don't* need a permit to have a child. Even convicted rapists and murderers are free to procreate and raise their own offspring without any government infringement or interference whatsoever.

4

OPENING NIGHT

EVERYONE LOVES THE grand opening of a restaurant. Everyone, that is, except for the owners, managers, bartenders, servers, cooks, and dishwashers. For VIPs and gate-crashers, it's all fun and games as food and booze are "on the cuff." For the most part, because it is almost impossible to please a high-end crowd, they go off into the night bad-mouthing the restaurant, never to return—until you throw another free party.

As the veteran of six restaurant grand opening fetes, I strongly suggest to all those about to flip their first burger that they skip the party and focus on preparing the restaurant to open in a calm, logical, professional manner. Most new owners rationalize an opening night shindig by envisioning a press bonanza and telling themselves that silent partners need a big bash to celebrate their brand-new toy. Neither idea could be further from the truth. The serious food press usually waits until the new place has been open for at least a month before rushing to judgment. The silent partners can wait and have a bunch of little mini-parties once the joint is open.

The page-sixers and the paparazzi may column-drop you in the morning paper—but you can book it that the ink won't flatter you. Moreover, after you've pulled three consecutive all-nighters preparing, right down to the last-minute paint or tile job in the rest rooms, your guests will trash the place.

Here's another good reason not to waste your time on an opening night party: money. The festivities are very expensive, simply because there are no revenues, and between the food, booze, and labor, costs can be staggering. The opening night party at Mickey Mantle's cost $25,000, plus the cost of replacing everything that was stolen or broken, including plates, ashtrays, and silverware. That money would have been better spent on an advertising schedule or to start a rainy-day payroll fund.

Mickey Mantle's opened February 5, 1988, with an opening night party. Several dark clouds floated over the event. First and foremost was that Mickey didn't know who to bring to the party: his wife, Merlyn, or his "agent," Greer Johnson. It was one or the other. Mickey wrestled with the decision for weeks. Merlyn was adamant about attending. She felt that as the mother of his four sons, she deserved to be there. Meanwhile Greer, like a custodian at the circus cleaning elephant poop, had spent years babysitting Mickey—following Mickey hither and thither on damage control—and she felt she had paid her dues and was as worthy of opening night attendance as anyone else.

Mickey chose Greer under massive pressure and told his wife he was going solo, because what with the expected crush of humanity and all, he didn't think the place would be safe for women and children. I don't know if she bought this flimsy explanation, but ultimately, Merlyn was out and Greer was in. Many months later, when

Mickey finally brought his wife in to see the place, an awkward situation ensued.

"Hello again!" one of the investors' wives said to her. "You look great! I haven't seen you since the opening."

Mickey was busted, and Merlyn bawled him out in the courtyard behind the restaurant. The next day, I got a call from Mickey's lawyer, Roy True, with a simple directive: "Mickey's not comfortable with that particular investor being in the deal." He explained that if I wanted Mickey's continued support in the venture, I would have to find a way to buy the rogue partner out posthaste. By the end of the week, we did so—but at a tidy premium.

A couple of days later, Greer demanded to meet with me privately in my basement office, where she declared that unless I paid her a hefty annual consulting fee, Mickey would never set foot in the restaurant again. After agonizing for a few days, I took a calculated risk by reporting the details of the conversation to Mickey.

When I approached him, he reached down and gave my nuts a perfunctory squeeze—a gesture that would become his standard greeting for me. Ignoring the burst of pain, I plunged right into my story about Greer trying to extort money under the guise of a consulting fee. He listened for only a few seconds before interjecting: "Fuckin' Greer. She's way too *glommy*." It was a word he often used to describe hangers-on and freeloaders.

"I'm about to dump her," he continued. "When she begs you for money, just nod your head up and down and say you'll think about it, but don't do it. If you give that glommy bitch any money, I really won't ever set foot in this place again."

Let's see . . . do I listen to Mickey, or do I listen to Greer? Mickey or Greer? I went with Mickey.

The biggest headache was the guest list. At that time, the place held about 300 people if you stuffed them in like sardines. The initial guest list contained 200 names—mostly friends and family of the partners. Then there was a secondary guest list of every journalist and celebrity on the face of the earth. We threw a lot of money at a PR firm to manage the mayhem, but every day the ditzy account rep called with another RSVP from some B-list journalist who simply had to attend.

The guest list began to multiply out of control, and there was nothing we could do about it. It would have been unthinkable to *un*-invite people, and I hadn't even counted the dozens of professional gate-crashers who would connive their way in the front door or through the cracks in the walls. All the while, Mickey hounded me relentlessly: "Make sure there're no more 'n 200 people in here on openin' naht," he kept saying. "Other-wahz, I'm outta here."

My new mantra became, "To the best of my knowledge, there will be no more than 200 guests."

"Okay, pard," he would say, staring holes into me as if to warn: *You better not be bullshitting me.*

The party was set to kick off at seven o'clock on that frigid February evening. Icy winds pummeled the front door, howling to be let in. Guess who else wanted in? The A-list celebs, reporters, and friends of the Mick who were freezing their asses off in a line that stretched all the way to the Plaza Hotel at the other end of the block. No one who actually mattered could get past the entry-level PR princesses who were guarding the door.

Here's who did get in: every freeloader in New York City, as well as their friends, relatives, and neighbors. Here's who never made it inside: Dan Rather, Howard Cosell, Walter Cronkite, Hank Aaron, Bob Costas, Mayor Abe Beame, Governor Hugh Carey, Raquel Welch, the

Roger Maris family, and Mickey's ex-flame, Angie Dickinson. I spent most of the next day fielding phone calls from angry reps demanding to know why their clients had literally been left out in the cold.

Howard Cosell called personally and delivered the following message: "Without me, there would be no Mickey Mantle."

Worst of all, I had to face Mickey after breaking my maximum capacity promise.

"I thought you told me there would only be 200 people," he roared.

"But Mickey," I pleaded, grasping at straws, "there only *were* 200."

"Horseshit," he said, and went on to explain how he'd been jostled and poked by throngs of crazed "guests" begging for autographs. He ended up slipping out the back with Billy Martin and bar hopping next door to the Helmsley Park Lane's upstairs lounge where the two of them closed the place.

The PR people counted every body that crossed the threshold that evening. Somehow, 850 people had managed to attend the party, almost four times our capacity as dictated by the fire code. At the end of the evening, I surveyed the wreckage and took a mental inventory of stolen plates, ashtrays, and anything else that wasn't nailed down. We were supposed to open for lunch the next day, but it took a full week to reconstruct and restock the restaurant and get ready for paying customers. All this extra time and effort translated into oodles of lost revenue.

The combined input of all the so-called journalists who were supposedly covering the event was sparse at best: a few pictures of Mickey with Billy Martin and Greer Johnson, and more than a few "love" letters from gossip columnists who couldn't get in or couldn't get close enough to the bar to order a drink. They also got nothing to eat because the gate-crashing pros positioned themselves right outside the kitchen door—the better to snatch up the hors d'oeuvres before the legitimate guests could.

As the restaurant neared its twentieth anniversary, I briefly considered throwing a huge bash to commemorate the milestone. However, after just a few seconds of careful consideration, I decided that I would be better served going home that evening to read to my kids and tuck them in.

5

CHEF SHAKEDOWN

NINE OUT OF TEN restaurants go belly-up within the first year. Even if a new restaurant outlives the astronomical failure rate, it must go through an agonizing "shakedown" period of six to eight months during which management attempts to identify the bad apples and then weed them out in order to assemble a team of "keeper" employees. Many executive chefs and general managers will not accept jobs at new restaurants because if the restaurant doesn't become successful in a hurry, they can kiss their new job good-bye.

Chefs are particularly hard to hire and even harder to keep. Either they can't cook or they can't manage a kitchen, or both. In any event, they tend to be riddled with personal problems, ranging in severity from anger management issues to drug addiction to kleptomania to bestial sodomy. The rate of substance abuse among chefs is the highest in any profession. The combination of late hours, infernally hot kitchens, easy access to booze, and the constant company of nubile young waitresses mix about as well as the ingredients in a Molotov cocktail.

Our first chef flat out had no idea how to cook. His barbequed chicken consisted of a boneless chicken breast with a blob of ketchup on top. I didn't keep him around long enough to find out what particular brand of sociopath he was. Chef number two described himself as "major," having worked in many prestigious New York eateries including the 21 Club and Gianni's, a once-hot, Upper East Side *ristorante*. Robert was a dead ringer for Bluto, of Popeye fame. The stubble on his scalp, face, and chest made up a matching set, and he carried a one-hundred-pound beer-belly on pencil-thin legs. The sheer mechanics of it all were mind-boggling. Worse yet was his acne; the term *pizza face* must have been coined for this beast of a man. In general, the best way to describe him would be "grossly unappetizing," an unfortunate trait for anyone in the culinary arts. In his brief tenure at Mickey's, he not only raised our food cost to 75 percent of our gross sales, but he also managed to repulse everyone he encountered with his crude antics—scaring off vendors, customers, and staff members alike.

Under Chef Robert's jurisdiction, the kitchen was always in the throes of chaos. Every time I passed through, the floor would be littered with garbage. Servers begged for their way-overdue entrees as a five-man line of amigos scrambled between the pantry, grill, fryer, sauté, and oven, engaging in their national pastime: insulting each other and span-oodling the apron-clad *chicas* as they lingered in the service area.

Suffice it to say that kitchen chatter is like a meeting of the Pan-American Congress on deviant human sexuality. One by one, the member nations take the floor. It usually begins when a waitress enters the kitchen, and it goes something like this:

EL SALVDOR: Me gustaría cojer ese mico.

EQUADOR: A ti no te gusta porque eres puto maricôn.

DOMINICAN REPUBLIC: De que tu hablas, si tu estabas maman-dome la pinga anoche.

VENESUELA: De verdad, Alfredo, te gusta mamar pinga.

MEXICO: Si, el estubo conmigo anoche mamando los huevos.

PUERTO RICO: Porque tu no te doblas ahora y te dejas piscar por el culo?

EL SALVADOR (again): Si tuvieras un million de dolares lo haria.

(Another waitress enters the kitchen.)

HONDURAS: Me gustariá poner la pinga en medio de sus tetas y venirme ensima de su cara.

But back to our chef: most chefs would expedite and sauté from behind the line in order to lower the payroll, but Robert's corpulence ruled this out for him, so, in turn, he made it impossible for anyone broader than Twiggy to shimmy past him on either his starboard or port sides in our crowded, narrow New York City kitchen.

I had just rushed upstairs from my basement office, and the only way from the basement to the floor is directly through the kitchen, where Mt. Robert stood in all his gory glory. When I reached the roadblock that was Robert, he made no effort to let me pass. Rather, with his feet planted, he turned to me amid a symphony of salsa music and pornographic kitchen chatter and bellowed, "Big dogs give the best head!"

"What?" I asked, totally perplexed by his bizarre declaration.

"I said, BIG DOGS GIVE THE BEST HEAD," he roared, thrusting a meaty paw into his blood-and-guts-stained chef's coat. He then pulled out a series of Polaroids and clipped them to the dupe board. The photos depicted three naked women gleefully accepting cunnilingus from hounds of various sizes and breeds. He went on to describe a ménage à trois involving him, one of the canines pictured, and a female chef from a well-known, *New York Times* four-star-rated restaurant.

He paused for a moment before producing another picture from his uniform. "This one's the best," he said, plucking the beloved snapshot from its hiding place and brandishing it theatrically between his index finger and thumb. It pictured a large, red Irish setter going down on an equally redheaded woman. "Ohhhhh, my," Robert sighed rapturously, "that dog sure likes to eat pussy!" Giggling like a schoolgirl, he grabbed a dinner napkin and polished the precious photo with small circular motions before tucking it safely back into his jacket.

He was the veteran of five marriages and bragged of countless liaisons between man, woman, and beast. Robert's fifth and current wife was the Olive Oyl to his Bluto. Her resemblance to the cartoon character was uncanny. She even dressed the part by pairing long, schoolmarmish skirts with gunboat shoes and tying her black hair into a tight bun at the nape of her neck like some sort of gothic ballerina. She also happened to be a blatantly anorexic skeleton of a woman who earned a living as a social worker. At about five foot five, she couldn't have weighed more than eighty-five pounds—roughly the equivalent of one of her husband's hefty man-tits. The two of them shared a modest one-bedroom love nest in the West Village.

At this time, we had several kitchen interns from The New York Restaurant School apprenticing at Mantle's. One such intern was the spitting image of Chef Robert in drag. As Mickey put it, "You couldn't even *drink* her purdy." She had morbid obesity in common with Robert, who, aside from being a dog aficionado, was a great lover of "fat broads," as he called them, and prided himself on the art of "bottom fishing."

"When you get to a bar," he counseled, "just make a beeline for the fattest, ugliest broad and you'll score every time. Go ugly, early." Gee, why hadn't I thought of that myself?

The tubby intern seemed to fancy Robert, and sure enough, romance soon blossomed between the two hulking forms in chef whites. It was a coital union that would make even the nonsqueamish squirm.

One time, following a weekday afternoon tryst at Robert's apartment, the intern left her king-sized panties between the sheets of his marital bed. After an honest day's work of shrinking heads at the clinic, Robert's beanpole wife came home to discover the oversize evidence there, between her very own paisley-print sheets. Robert was busted, big-time.

When I arrived at work the next morning, I found a sobbing, red-eyed, unshowered and unshaven Chef Robert in my office. As I struggled to unearth the source of his misery, his weeping turned into a shortness of breath, which led to a call to 911, as Robert had previously suffered several heart attacks. Minutes later, as the paramedics wheeled him out of the restaurant on a stretcher, he told me that he had returned home the night before to a completely bare apartment, which he described as "broom-clean." His wife had stripped their home of all their belongings and fled the building, never to be seen or heard from again.

Robert never returned to Mickey Mantle's, but lucky for us, his "highly trained" sous-chef was ready to step in and fill his shoes. Barry was a flamboyant, balding man in his forties with a Bozo-the-clown hairdo. His flaming hair matched his flaming mannerisms, made all the more peculiar by the jumbo-sized hearing aid he wore in his left ear and the exaggerated limp he had acquired from a childhood bout with polio. Worse yet, his hearing impairment begat him a larger-than-life whining lisp, which stuck out like a sore thumb among the din of salsa music and macho banter that always filled the kitchen.

"But Wobewt say-ed dat you gotta make da waviowi *wif* da winguini," he would wail to the tittering prep cooks. "Wobert say-ed da wat-tat-toowee goes wif da wigatoni, not da woast chicken!"

Everything anyone said or did in there was followed by "but Wobewt say-ed!" And everywhere he went, a wake of Hispanic kitchen staff would follow close behind, jovially mimicking his peculiar walk and talk. Barry didn't stay long enough to settle in as chef number three. Shortly thereafter, Robert was released from the hospital and Barry, true to form, followed him to his next gig like Sancho Panza and Don Quixote.

On deck was Artie, a tall, black-bearded man with zealous energy and boisterous confidence. After an uneventful first week as chef number three, during which he worked around the clock with maniacal fervor (he even pulled an all-nighter on Thanksgiving eve in order to cook all the turkeys), Artie went missing after his shift on Friday. He didn't make it home to his wife that evening, and he remained at large for the entire weekend, missing his shift both days. The police were notified about the AWOL chef, whose wife bombarded me with frantic phone calls. Late Monday afternoon, just when I was starting to entertain the thought of an alien abduction, a sheepish Chef Artie tiptoed in the front door. I greeted him and ushered him downstairs to my office for an immediate huddle.

He looked ghostly and ghastly, his pale skin blotched with flaky, red patches. His eyes were bloodshot and fully dilated, the irises like two black pearls tossing on a red tide.

"Bill," he began shakily, "you're not gonna believe what happened."

He was right—I didn't.

Artie, it seems, had left on Friday evening, stopping at an ATM machine on his way to the Port Authority bus station where he usually caught the bus home to Jersey. He claimed he had been accosted at gunpoint near the cash machine, but alas, his account was tapped out; he had nothing to offer the thieves but his paycheck and a bus ticket to Nutley. Unsatisfied, they jabbed a gun into the small of his back and dragged him to their Times Square hovel. There, they bound and gagged him, holding him until Monday so that he could cash his paycheck and buy his release. According to Artie, they had only taken his gag out long enough to force him to snort a line of coke now and again. This last piece of information struck me as the most bizarre.

Artie went on to explain that on Sunday, in the middle of the night when all the cokeheads were asleep (yeah, right), he had managed to pry himself loose from his shackles and escape the squalid drug den. Apparently, he had sold this yarn to his wife, but with me it was no sale.

Make way for Connor, chef number four. A folk-singing chef with a long, bushy ponytail, Connor had served as executive chef in several famous New York eateries, including my brother David's Manhattan Market restaurant. A learned and creative culinary ace with taste buds still intact, the other cooks looked up to him, and even the servers thought of him fondly.

Connor's own fondness for alcohol turned out to be his Achilles' heel. His breath always smelled either of vodka, or of vodka mixed with minty mouthwash, but he seemed to get the job done. He was that old contradiction in terms: a functioning alcoholic. Early on in his tenure, I tweaked him about his drinking, and he poo-pooed me. When he continued to arrive at work shit-faced, I confronted him and suggested that he had a problem.

"No, I don't," he countered. "I'm a social drinker. And besides, it doesn't interfere with my work, so what's it to you?"

He had a point. For the first time in the short history of my restaurant, the food was coming out of the kitchen on time and tasting great. I let him slide for the time being.

Shortly thereafter, Connor started missing shifts and getting sloppy on the line, staggering around in a vodka-drenched haze and mumbling incoherently to no one in particular. This time around, I bypassed Connor and called his live-in girlfriend to express my concern.

"Connor is *not* an alcoholic," she argued, "but the job at Mickey's is so stressful that I have to mix him a pitcher of Bloody Mary's just to get him out of bed and off to work in the morning."

Chef number five was Troy, who was fresh from a three-star restaurant in Santa Cruz or Santa Barbara or Santa whatever. He wanted to "Californianize" the menu by adding avocado and pineapple to dishes like chicken-fried steak, and he could be found during our most busy luncheons stripped down to the waist, playing Frisbee in Central Park. After spending several weeks improving his alfresco Frisbee skills, Troy found himself out of a job.

"Whatever," he scoffed, rolling his eyes like an insolent teenager. "I really need to be working in, like, a *fine-dining* restaurant. Like, bye." And he pranced out the door, Frisbee in hand.

Chef number six was Michael Salmon, a graduate of the Culinary Institute of America, and married with two small daughters. Much to my delight, Michael fixed the food and refurbished the staff at Mickey's in under a fortnight. At his last job, he was the number two to Anne Rosensweig at Arcadia, a highly publicized, four-star, New York City restaurant. Arcadia had also received top-notch ratings from the Zagat guide, unlike Mickey Mantle's, which had scored a paltry twelve points (one point less than Burger Heaven). We weren't a twenty, but we certainly deserved a solid fifteen or sixteen points by any reasonable standards. I was acquainted with Tim Zagat from my days at The New York Restaurant School, and I knew that his knee-jerk reaction was to blow off sports bars and otherwise nonchic venues. In fact, Zagat guide ratings are supposed to be based on customer reviews, but (although there is no proof) an acquaintance of mine who worked at Zagat alleged that he takes a red pen to the actual results and alters them to reflect his personal opinion before going to press. (One year, I had solicited over one hundred favorable reviews of Mickey Mantle's from friends and family; our Zagat's rating didn't change.) I intended to win him over.

I invited Tim to sample the food from our great new chef, whose name I omitted. Tim reluctantly accepted my invitation, and when he arrived at Mantle's, Michael proceeded to pump out three of Arcadia's signature dishes and serve them on Mantle's plates. Mr. Zagat gave the food a cursory taste and turned up his nose.

"This food is just not good," he declared.

"What about it isn't good?" I asked him.

"It's just *not good*," he replied stubbornly, like a child defending his own faulty reasoning with "just because." My theory had been accurate; same food, same chef, different setting, poor reviews. Another arrogant food-phony exposed with his pants down at his ankles.

Several days later, my phone rang at 6:00 A.M. I hadn't had my first cup of coffee and I was slow on the uptake. I reached gingerly for the phone.

"LIEDERMAN," yelled the voice on the other end, "this is Imus!"

I flipped over in bed and rubbed my eyes as it hit me that I was being crank-called live on the *Imus in the Morning* show on WFAN radio.

"Tell me something," Imus continued, "why would a chef at Arcadia leave to become chef at a greasy spoon like Mickey's?"

No match for Imus at any hour, I groped for a response and came up short—which didn't even matter, because Imus's famous mouth was in full working order.

"Not exactly a brilliant career move, is it? Kind of like Mickey being sent back to Triple-A. Why'd he do it, Liederman?"

Desperate to stop the bleeding, I replied, "For the money, Imus, for the money."

"Yeah, it's always about the money," he quipped, and promptly hung up on me.

Michael left after a three-year tenure that ended with a bitter divorce from his wife; he was spending too many late nights at Mickey's taking "inventory" in his office, which he liked to do with his face nestled between the bottle-blond bartender's beautiful breasts.

Michael stepped aside for his sous-chef, Randy Pietro, aka chef number seven. In the world of the Mick, lucky seven had to be a keeper, and he was. Randy had also graduated from the Culinary Institute of America. He spent fourteen years as executive chef at Mickey Mantle's before opening his own place, Latitude 40, in Point Pleasant. He is also happily married with two kids and a two-car garage on the Jersey Shore. For the duration of his tenure, he never drank or did drugs, and he never called in sick. To this day, he remains a perfectly well-adjusted individual, which may be the hardest part of this entire story to believe, if you're in the biz.

6

RESTAURANT RESUMÉS

FINDING COMPETENT, honest restaurant employees is no easy task. I believe all restaurant resumés should come with the following disclaimer: Much of the previous employment information appearing on this document has been altered. Many, if not all, of the references do not actually exist. Names have been imagined, places have been changed, and this document generally bears no truthful information about the applicant.

In the course of my food service career, I have sorted through stacks of resumés, and it never ceased to astonish me what people will write on these things. Applicants will go out of their way to impart random and unnecessary information that can only cause their resumé to wind up in the trash. Here are a few gems from a want ad for servers on Craigslist.

Ms. Pinky Moore
Work Experience in New York City!
Indian Tag Restaurant, Divan Grill, Baluchi Indian Restaurant.

(Into the trash. Haiku format aside, who refers to themselves as "Ms." on a resumé? Why not go all out and dub yourself Madam Pinky? She could set up a tent and read palms in the kiddie play area.)

Michael Palmer

Please excuse the jumbled format of this resumé, due to the cut and paste, considering the fact that few people accept attachments.

(Anyone who can't take the time to organize their resumé into some understandable format can't take the time to service the customers properly.)

Chaya M. Glick

Experience: waitress in Jerusalem, Israel, 2002–2004
Interests: speaks Hebrew fluently
Objective: get job in borough of Manhattan

(The Hebrew would have come in handy with Mickey, who made dozens of appearances at Bar Mitzvahs, but still butchered the word. The closest he ever came was "Bark Matzah." One of my favorite Mickey Moments occurred when my longtime accountant, Irwin Kalmanowitz, who is an Orthodox Jew, asked me to have baseballs signed for his sons, Yehuda and Moishe. Upon hearing these names, or at least the way I mispronounced them, Mickey started bellowing like a moose on crack. Yahoooooooda, Yahoooooooda, Yahoooooooda, he repeated over and over again. When the laughs died down, Mickey signed the two balls to Yehuda and Moishe, but only after four balls had to be tossed in the trash before he got both names right. Almost twenty years later, I'm sure the Kalmanowitz sons still display them proudly.)

Kenneth Kessler

About me: In my spare time, I enjoy reading, bicycle riding, kayaking, tap dancing, knitting, and watching the Wizard of Oz.

('Nuff said.)

Rita P. Goldstein

Professional cafeteria worker

(Can't you almost see the hairnet? Despite what Tim Zagat may say, this ain't no fucking cafeteria. Lunch ladies need not apply.)

Kristen Allison Wilks

Technician associate in dental implant & cosmetic surgery

(An out-of-work oral surgeon? Where do I even begin?)

Petra Romanska

Interests: Kurgan State University, Kurgan, Russia

(Um . . . okay, this woman's *interests* are Kurgan State University? I mean, I know Kurgan State is the Harvard of the Soviet Union, but c'mon.)

Jade Pinero

Employment: Snooky's Restaurant & Pub, Brooklyn, New York, 2002–present
Doggy Heaven, Valley Stream, New York, 1989–1991

(Are we talking about a woman, or a dog?)

Nassir Naciri
- King Falafel on Third
- Bellboy of Atlas Asni Hotel, Morocco
- Diplomat in Morocco

(Why the hell is a diplomat looking for work in a restaurant? And, one might ask, what kind of diplomat moonlights as a bellboy?)

Shahid H. Malik
Education 1999–2000, Thomas Moore College, Merrimack, NH
- Liberal Arts
- Completed freshman year

(If you've only completed your freshman year, don't tell me about it. It makes you sound like a quitter. Either fudge it and say you graduated, or leave the education entry blank.)

Bitsy Felicia Goldfarb
Work experience: Nutritional social worker @ the Hebrew Home for the Aged, Riverdale, NY

(Thanks anyway, Bitsy, but the last thing I need is some vegan health nut asking customers if they *really* want that chicken-fried steak.)

Holly Holgate
Hello, my name is Holly Holgate, and I am an actress here in NYC, which basically means I need to get a J-O-B! I am outgoing friendly hardworking and experienced saver.
Serving experience:

Hooters, Wethersfield, CT, 860–563–8083 and ask for "Spankie"
Other:
Typing, good people skillz, special skillz, actor/singer
*acting resumé upon request.

(Holly, when can you start?)

Vadim Aleksandrov
7/2004–present: Identities Model Management, 244 5th Ave,
New York, NY 10001
MODEL
Model in runway shows and photo shoots
8/2004–present: Oliver Cheng Catering, 495 Broadway, 2nd Fl,
New York, NY 10012
CATER WAITER
Serving hors d'oeuvres and drinks
Facilitating return of customers by interpersonal skills.

(Vadim, my main man, what else do cater waiters do besides
serve hors d'oeuvres and drinks? What *exactly* do you mean by
"interpersonal skills"?)

Herman F. Boot
Health: Excellent

(Herman, nobody asked you about your health. To do so
would be pointless. How else would an applicant answer this self-
imposed question . . . Health: piss poor? Health: I have the
bubonic plague? leprosy? a touch of Tourette's syndrome? Or how
about, Health: I'm writing this resumé from my death bed?)

Maria Santa Rosa

Brooklyn, NY

I am seeking a wateress job at your resturant. I once worked at houligan's in the empire state bilding, but to be honest, I gave it up after 6 munths because a guy offered me a lot more to dance at a club on west 46th street. It was a topless place and the pay was grate, but I got fired for being caught doing drugs backstage, and really, what do they expect from a topless dancer, it was total bullshit. How the fuk can you get throguh 4 shifts anyway without doing some kind of drug, you know? Anyway I am good wuith people, I wont do drugs at your place, and I am available right away. What kind of uniforms do you have to ware?

(If you are going to use the F-word in your application for employment, you might at least spell it correctly.)

And the servers are just the tip of the iceberg. What about the managers, the chefs, the stewards, and every other position you have to fill in order to staff a viable NYC restaurant? In the earliest days of Mickey Mantle's, before we had hired a single server or even broken ground on the construction site, I hired the restaurant's very first employee: a building contractor.

As every builder in town wanted to build the house that Mantle built, I waded through a stack of construction proposals the size of *War and Peace* before I was able to narrow it down to three or four viable applicants. A couple of large construction companies boasted glowing recommendations from big-name, big-time restaurants, but they were currently juggling several different projects. We were on a tight schedule, and I needed the undivided attention of that one, perfect-ten of a contractor.

Whomever he was, he and his posse of subcontractors were going to become my constant companions on the job site until the ribbon-cutting.

Our construction was slated to commence in October of 1988 in order to make a February 5th opening night. Actually, it was February 5th or bust because of Mickey's busy schedule.

One morning during the grueling selection process, I was sitting in the front window of Les Tuileries, the defunct French bistro that was slated for reincarnation as Mickey Mantle's. Suddenly, a Harley-Davidson roared up to the curb. The rider dismounted his hog and ripped off his helmet to reveal a chrome-dome adorned with a tiny, platinum-blond ponytail that clung pathetically to the nape of his pale pink neck. A large diamond stud impaled his meaty left earlobe. The look was equal parts repulsive and impressive; it was like the guy had one-upped Mr. Clean. But I had scarcely had time to notice any of this before he began rapping on the storefront window about three inches away from my face.

"*Hello*," he yelled, "Mark—the builder—here. Are you the guy who's building this joint?"

"Yes . . ." I confessed, backing away from the glass.

"Yeah, well I heard through the grapevine that you're looking for a contractor," he said, letting himself through the French doors.

"It depends," I told him.

"Depends on what?"

"Depends on whether or not you have time to focus on the job."

"Yeah, yeah, I just finished my last restaurant and I'm wide open."

"What restaurant?" I wanted to know.

"Home on the Range."

"What other restaurants are you building now?"

"Other restaurants? What the hell is your name?"

"Bill Liederman."

"Yeah, Bill Liederman, lemme make this clear," he said, before launching into the first in a long line of bold-faced lies. "I'm a mom-'n'-pop operation. I only take one job at a time."

"Well, if you're Mom, then who's Pop?"

"Fuck you," he snapped. "I'm Pop, and Mom is none of your fucking business."

I was starting to like the guy. I envisioned him as a tough, no-nonsense field general who would go to the steel-toed boot in order to get a job done on time.

"Got a resumé, Mark?"

"What the fuck for?" he asked, knitting his pale white brow.

"So I can check your references," I admitted, because I didn't much care where he'd gone to college or what his hobbies might be. The only relevant factors were which restaurants he had built and how they had turned out.

"Here are my references," he replied, and proceeded to rattle off half a dozen big-name jobs.

I knew these restaurants and their owners from my days at The New York Restaurant School. In fact, some of them happened to be NYRS graduates.

"I assume everyone on that list will tell me you're the second coming of The Lord Jesus H. Christ," I sighed.

"Of course, they will. Why the fuck else would I have chosen them? So they can tell you I'm a lying, thieving scumbag?"

He had a point.

"Tell you what," I said. "Give me the name of one restaurant owner who hates you so much he would kill you if it was legal."

"Bob Johnson," he answered without a moment's thought. "I built his place on Third Avenue. He'd blow my brains out in a Miami minute."

"Give me his phone number," I demanded.

"No problem," he said, reciting it from memory. "I'll never get that one out of my head."

I knew he was going to call this Johnson guy for a heads-up as soon as I was out of earshot, so I picked up the phone and began dialing on the spot.

"Mind if I call him now?"

"Shit, no," he said. "Why the fuck do I care? If I get this job, fine. If not, that's fucking fine, too. There's always another fucking restaurant to fucking build."

Bob Johnson answered his phone on the first ring.

"Hi Bob, this is Bill Liederman, founder and former executive director of The New York Restaurant School."

"We're not hiring," he barked and hung up.

I hit the redial, and he answered again, this time with, "What?" instead of the standard hello.

"Don't hang up, I'm not looking for a job," I blurted, before he could write me off. "I'm getting ready to build Mickey Mantle's Restaurant on Central Park South and . . ."

"Wow," he squealed, "I love the Mick! How about an autograph?"

Finally, I had his full attention.

"What do you know about a contractor by the name of Mark Richards?" I asked.

"You *gotta* be kidding me," he howled. "If that jackass used me for a reference, he must have a fucking death wish. I'd sooner give a good recommendation for Adolph fucking Hitler."

"Care to elaborate?"

"Oh, Bill, I'd be more than *thrilled* to elaborate. The guy's a fucking pathological liar. He almost ruined me. You'd be crazy to hire that sack of shit."

"What did he lie about?" I asked.

"Everything," Johnson screamed. "We wound up with a six-month delay and a half-a-million-dollar overrun. They should really pull that cocksucker's contracting license."

"So you like him?"

"*Like* him? What the *fuck*? I don't have time for this cocka-mamy bullshit. Good-bye, Bill." And he was gone.

"Well, Mark," I said, dropping the phone onto the desk, "I'm at a loss. You may be a pathological lair, but at least you're honest about it. You're hired."

We haggled over the financials, and just as he was leaving, Mickey walked past him on the way in.

"Ah don't know who the fuck that guy was, but the ponytail and the earrings have got to go."

"Don't worry," I said, "he's not a server. He's a contractor."

"Ah don't care who the fuck he is. I never want to see his sissy-assed face again."

Mark turned out to be a real Jekyll-and-Hyde type of contractor. An ex-cokehead and booze addict, he attended daily AA and NA meetings to keep him on the twelve-step path. Beneath the gruff exterior, he actually had a sweet disposition, but he was given to the mood swings of a dry drunk. To this by-hook-or-by-crook of a man, lies were but tools of the trade. Each day at the job site, he would regale me with what I dubbed, "the excuse du jour."

The man couldn't breathe without slightly fudging the truth. Moreover, he fibbed in situations where the truth would actually have been more effective. To this day, I'm not quite convinced his name was Mark Richards. At Mickey's request he did make a few adjustments, such as nixing the ear-bling and hiding the ponytail with a Yankees cap. Best of all, he got the job done on time and under budget. Even Mickey agreed that the place looked fantastic.

Potential restaurant employees are particularly hard to get a grip on. They say that a restaurant manager is interrupted more times in a day than someone of any other profession, so the interview process gets seriously compromised by the need to focus on the disaster at hand. Excuse me, but I have to cut this short as the kitchen is on fire and the chef just pulled a knife on a waitress.

In this crazy business, if the applicant doesn't piss his or her pants, the best thing to do is to have them trail for a day to see if they can walk the floor, carry drinks, talk to customers, and not chew gum at the same time. For anyone who's ever wondered about the interview process, here is a small sample of the questions that restaurant applicants can expect to answer.

To a server: "How important is giving good service to you?"

Standard answer: "I am a people person, and people come first."

To a bartender: "Are you honest? Because I'm looking for an employee, not a partner."

Standard answer: "I've never stolen anything in my life, and I don't intend to start now. This job is too important to me."

To a manager: "Do you have a drinking or drug problem?"

Standard answer: "Absolutely not. This is a reputable establishment, and I would never dream of compromising your operation by drinking on the job." (Notice how the standard answer makes no mention of what drinking and drugging may take place before or after a shift.)

Second question to a manager: "If you have a problem with a server, how do you handle it?"

Standard answer: "I wait until there is a quiet moment, and then I pull the server aside and explain what needs to be done. I never, ever lose my temper on the floor. That would be unprofessional, particularly within the earshot of customers."

Quiet moment my ass. There's never a quiet moment. If you want a quiet moment, go work in a library. The reality is that I have never known a manager who adhered to this credo. It usually takes only a few shifts before they're reaming out bewildered servers in the middle of the dining room. *HEATHER! The next time you fuck up an order you're FIRED!* This usually results in tears, and the server is pulled off the floor until she can pull herself together. Or she up and quits.

In any case, staffing a restaurant is a real crapshoot. All things considered, you might as well pick your employees with a blindfold and darts.

7

JOHNNY SIDEBURNS

Mamas, don't let your babies grow up to be restaurant managers. What's wrong with being a cowboy, with plenty of sunshine and fresh country air in between Marlboros? Restaurant night manager is a far more perilous career choice.

For starters, your typical evening manager works six days a week from 2:00 p.m. to 2:00 a.m., or 3:00 to 3:00, depending on closing time. That leaves a maximum of one day off per nightmarish week. This day will probably fall between Monday and Thursday, when most people are chilling at home watching reality shows. As a result, the night manager falls out of synch (and out of touch) with the rest of the world. Friendships wane, and in the absence of peers, the much-anticipated off day is spent alone on the couch with booze, coke, pot, and whacking off to porn.

And that's just the day *off*. On workdays, 2:00 a.m. to 5:00 a.m. is party time. Night managers usually sneak a few pops at their own bars, snort a few lines, and then head out for an early morning of debauchery with some chefs. First come a series of local bars, and then on to the after-hours joints.

But the trouble doesn't end there. A nasty constellation of other perils awaits new night managers. In a sports bar, gambling addiction is a big one. You can tell if your manager is a compulsive gambler on his first night. If he stops and watches TV for more than thirty seconds in a row or asks customers the score, he's got at least a Ben Franklin or two riding on the game.

We once had an evening manager named Steve. He was a compulsive gambler who majored in pro hockey. He was also a compulsive booger-eater. Steve would stand at attention in the middle of the dining room, glued to a hockey game, fervently picking his nose for all to see. He wouldn't budge until his team scored, and then he'd switch the booger from his right index finger to his left before giving the air a victory punch with his right fist. Go Rangers!

Restaurant owners must hire with extreme care. Putting a compulsive gambler, drinker, drug user, or kleptomaniac in charge of a big-time restaurant is a big-time mistake. Unfortunately, even if your night manager doesn't start out with bad habits, he or she will likely develop them lickety-split. The trick is to hire the applicant who'll last the *longest*, as only a rare few can avoid these vices altogether.

During the interview process, I always ask potential managers up front about their vices. Of course, most of them deny any kind of chemical indulgence, but some of them spill their guts in the hopes of scoring brownie points for honesty. For example, one manager fessed up to having had a drinking problem that had stemmed from another, bigger issue: anger management. He went on to admit his involvement in countless barroom brawls at his previous workplaces. The last time he'd brawled, he took a shiv right in the gut, costing him most of his stomach. The near-fatal injury forced him to swear off booze and all-day buffets in favor of six tiny meals a day, which only made him hungrier and angrier. He had begun seeing an anger management counselor in the hopes of breaking the vicious cycle once and for all.

I couldn't resist his sincerity, so I gave him a shot at the gig. Two weeks later, we hosted a closed-circuit event for one of the early Mike Tyson fights. As per usual, a series of brawls broke out among the punters and pundits at the bar. I had warned my pugilistic manager about the possible postfight fisticuffs, but when the inevitable occurred, instead of breaking it up, he piled right on and joined in the fray. The hostess paged me, and I ran upstairs from my office to find my new night manager sitting on top of one customer with another one in a half nelson.

I got some of the kitchen guys to help me pull him off the customers, and then I saw him to the door.

"Sorry, Bill," he offered on his way out, "I guess I just couldn't handle it."

To replace him, I hired Doug Van Horn, who'd played sixteen seasons with the New York Giants and was the offensive team captain in 1974. After his football career ended, Doug and a partner had opened The Front Row, a sports bar of their own within a long touchdown pass of Giants Stadium in East Rutherford, New Jersey.

When I got his resumé in the mail, I wasted no time bringing him in for an interview. He was about forty pounds below playing weight and looked like a mere mortal without the bulk of his pads. I hired him as my new daytime manager at an annual salary of $55,000. Of course, this was peanuts compared to what he'd made as a New York Giant, but he didn't seem to mind. Each day, he reported to work with a big smile on his face, as if to say: *I'm happy to be here, I'm happy to be alive. Let's go get 'em!* Then he'd call the entire back-of-house and kitchen staff into a huddle for a preshift meeting. Although many employees spoke little or no English, he managed to communicate, and the huddle would break to clapping hands and chants of "clean, clean, CLEAN!" Doug would then release them to clean the entire restaurant in forty-five minutes.

Due to his postcareer weight loss, few Giants fans recognized him during the lunch shift, but those who did always had the same reaction: "Holy shit," they'd say. "You really are Doug Van Horn! Doug Van Horn of the New York Giants works at Mickey Mantle's!"

He was a good-looking bachelor. One day, when Doug was in the liquor room taking inventory, I heard sexy sounds coming from behind the heavy, metal door. I tip-toed in and found Doug doing the nasty doggie style with my assistant bookkeeper on top of a case of Bud Light.

Hanky panky aside, things were going great for Doug at his new job. The staff idolized him, and things were progressing nicely in his romance with the bookkeeper. Best of all, he was great at his job, and I decided to promote him to general manger at a nifty pay increase. However, when I called him into my office to pop the question, he simply said it was "time to move on." He had a very determined, settled look on his face, so I didn't try to argue. Just as suddenly as he had appeared on the scene, Doug vanished like disappearing ink.

The last manager I ever hired at Mickey's was a real charmer. His family had owned a series of Greek diners, so we'll call him Gus the Greek. Gus was an amiable guy with what turned out to be a nasty drinking problem.

"Do you drink?" I asked him during his interview.

"I don't have a drinking problem," he said, "but I do like to have one drink, after I lock the place up, just before I hit the road."

Translation: "My problem right now is that I need a drink in order to get through this interview. Once hired, I will drink throughout my shift and on into the wee hours of the night. At any given moment, I will be either *on* a bender or crawling out from under one. As a result, I will miss ten days in my first three months of employment at Mantle's."

Being wasted around so many attractive, young servers so much of the time inevitably leads to affairs between night managers and their crew. Once your night man starts servicing a server, he's toast. Nobody in his employ will ever take him seriously again, and he can rest assured that the entire staff will know, in six different languages, how he couldn't get it up—or keep it up—the night before.

Now your night man is at the mercy of that one special waitress. He knows that if he fires her, she'll sue for sexual harassment and win. Worse yet, she knows that he knows. With this unspoken arrangement intact, insubordination rules the day. Soon, she's coming in late, calling out sick, rewriting the schedule so that she and her friends can cherry-pick their shifts. This activity breeds jealousy among the other servers, spawning mutinous conditions on the floor.

Meanwhile, due to his compulsive gambling problem, your typical night manager begins to skim cash out of the drop in order to pay off his bookie. But he can only rip the house off a little bit at a time without upper management getting wise. The stress from mounting debt begins to unhinge him, so later that night, after losing all five of his bets (four of them in a miracle manner), the booze wears away his common sense and the next thing he knows, he's bought a bag of nose-candy with the money he stole earlier that evening. He snorts a few lines to bolster his nerve.

Now he feels like a real slick Rick, so after work, at the neighborhood haunt, he picks up a waitress he's been eyeing since he first saw her in her sexy number 7 jersey. Push comes to shove, and they end up pushing and shoving into each other back at his apartment.

Another time, I hired this young Texas guy whom I called Tex—night manager number 287 in fifteen years. Tex was around the same age as most of the servers at Mantle's, but he looked serious and had actually completed a four-year degree at Southwest Texas State (or wherever) with a major in hospitality.

"Welcome aboard," I told him. "Just promise me one thing."

"Sure," he agreed. "Anything, boss."

"As Mickey used to say, never, ever, ever ride the workhorses. I don't want any romantic melodrama between you and the servers. Is that understood?"

"Of course," he pledged, a somber look on his Texas Ranger face. "It's a deal."

Three weeks later, I caught wind of a dalliance between Tex and "Sally," a waitress who was supposedly engaged to her live-in boyfriend. Sally had already proven her loyalty several times over by bedding five waiters, a bartender, two waitresses, and a couple of cops on the beat. Tex turned out to be next in line when, one morning, they were seen stumbling out of a taxi together in front of Mantle's at 11:00 a.m. Fishy, because they lived on opposite ends of the park. Predictable, because they'd left together the night before.

When I confronted Tex about the alleged tryst, he was mortified.

"Ah messed up," he moaned. "Ah promise I'll never do it agay-un."

But once was enough for me. Next!

The only night manager I've ever had who didn't drink, do drugs, gamble compulsively, fight, or fornicate with the staff was Ross Cafaro. Ross was a small-town boy from just outside Pittsburgh, and aside from a bong hit or two in college, or a bit too much bubbly on New Year's Eve, he was as clean as a hound's tooth.

He was no Rhodes Scholar, but he was appealing in his simplicity: honest, humble, hardworking. He was a handsome man—tall, fit, and well dressed—but he lacked that city-guy edge that gets city guys laid. He was far too vanilla for your typical New York City gal. Then, one day, his favorite wristwatch broke and he took it to a cute, closet-sized repair shop in the West Village, near his apartment.

The shop was owned and operated by a Hungarian beauty who had been looking for a man like Ross since her arrival in the States eight years before. On finding him, she swallowed him down like Ms. Pac-Man. She even *looked* like Ms. Pac-Man, with a large, lace bow perched daintily atop her carefully coiffed and frosted locks. Very Like-a-Virgin, circa 1984.

Due to some pesky green card problems, she needed to get married in a hurry. She also "needed" to live in a certain building, with certain amenities, in a certain area of Brooklyn. She had a sexy accent and gorgeous, round, sparkling aquamarine eyes, and she looked great on his arm. So he caved in to all of her demands, including the shotgun wedding.

About a month after their honeymoon, Ross consulted me about some marital problems he was facing. In addition to his wife's increasingly irrational behavior, he suspected that she was having an affair.

He hired a private dick, who came running back to him with a stack of glossy eight-by-tens picturing her playing tonsil hockey with a local crime boss by the moniker of "Johnny Sideburns" at a casino in Atlantic City. Ross's new wife was stepping out with a made man.

Before he could confront her, however, he received a telephone message from Mr. Sideburns. It went something like this: "Ross, this is Johnny Sides. Listen carefully: your marriage to Zsuzsanna is ovah. She's movin' in with *me*. You have twenty-four hours to get the hell outta town. After that, you bettah *hope* I nevah catch you in dis town after tomorrow."

"So what should I do?" Ross asked me.

"Get out of town now," I blurted. It pained me to say it, but I knew it was his only shot at survival. I took a day off to help him move and off he went, never to return. I don't know what became of the romance between Ms. Hungary and Sideburns, but Ross went home to Pittsburgh to care for his dying mother. In doing so, he met Claire, her personal nurse. They're now married with three great-looking kids. I know this because every holiday season, I get a portrait-studio family photo-card from the Cafaro clan. Ross always looks happy, and it just so happens that he no longer works in the restaurant business. Coincidence? I think not.

HOOK ME UP

SHORTLY AFTER MICKEY'S opened, I moved into a modest one-bedroom apartment at 40 Central Park South, directly above the restaurant. Because I was Mickey Mantle's partner, I attained instant BMOC status among the doormen and maintenance detail. The restaurant was the building's highest paying renter, and most of the staff were sports fans who hoped I could hook them up with Mickey's autograph and anything else they could glom. When I entered the plush, marble lobby, they would stand at attention and salute me as if I were the President of the United States. It was great; sometimes I could almost hear "Hail to the Chief" playing in the background. One of the younger guys was called Ricardo, which suited him perfectly. He and Desi Arnaz were separated at birth.

On the evening I moved in, I finished up at the restaurant and headed home for my virgin slumber in the new crib. When I reached the lobby, Ricardo was behind the desk, on sentry duty.

"Welcome home, Mr. Liederman," he greeted me. "Is there anything I can do for you this evening?"

"No thanks, Ricardo; I'm cool," I assured him. "But from now on, I want us to communicate with hand signals, so when I come through the lobby at night, you'll know exactly what I need. You know, just between us guys. They tell me the walls have ears in this place."

"No problem," he agreed. "Show me the signals." He said, as serious as a heart attack.

"Well," I explained, "if I touch my left hand like *this*," exaggerating the motion, slapping my left wrist like a baseball skipper signaling a left-hander in the bullpen, "it means I want you to send a gorgeous young hooker up to my apartment. But if I touch my right hand like *this*," reversing the procedure, "it means that I want you to send up the hottest waitress from the restaurant."

He seemed totally unfazed, so I reached down and grabbed my balls with both hands, à la Roseanne, and gave him a sexy smile.

"Lastly, Ricardo, if I grab at my nuts real hard, like *this*, it means that I want *you* to come up. Got it?"

"Okay, Mr. Liederman," Ricky replied without missing a beat. "I'm your man."

In the elevator, I laughed my way through the fourteen-story ride.

The next evening, when I got to the lobby, Ricardo was manning his post. As I moved toward him, I signaled to the bullpen for a left-hander, and Ricardo winked his confirmation. Not a word was spoken as I boarded the elevator.

Waiting for me upstairs was Sari, my twenty-two-year-old girl-friend, a junior at Hampshire College. She was curled up on the couch, crocheting or sculpting or engaging in some equally crunchy type of arts and crafts project, sipping Celestial Seasonings Tummy Mint Tea.

We were settling in for a movie when suddenly the doorbell rang three times quickly. Sari had mentioned having ordered food up from Mickey's, so we both figured it was the delivery guy at the door. I opened it without looking or asking, and there, standing in front of me, was a buxom young woman with long, silky red hair and a milky-white Irish complexion. She looked quite fetching in a low-cut, red halter-dress and a mink, or some other pelt of a small dead animal, wrapped about her shoulders. She smiled at me with wide, brown eyes and wiggled the tips of her fingers in a girlish *hello*.

"Ricardo told me you wanted to see somebody," she whispered, stepping with one foot into the apartment.

"Bill, is that my delivery?" Sari chirped from the living room. I could hear her padding toward the door to see what was up.

"I got it, Baby," I hollered over my shoulder, ushering my visitor back out the door.

"Listen," I whispered, "this is all a big mistake. It's just a practical joke I have going with Ricardo, and I didn't mean . . ." I fumbled for words to make her go quietly, and fearing that Sari would bust through the door at any moment, I finally settled for a less-is-more approach: "It was just a joke, you know? I'm sorry."

Nothing could have prepared me for her reaction, which went something like this: "You fucking asshole cocksucker-motherfucker cocksucking bastard! You think what I do is a fucking joke, you motherfucking cocksucking Jew-bastard son of a bitch?! FUCK YOU!"

At this point, she was screaming at the tippy-top of her very substantial lungs. All I needed was for my brand-new neighbors to overhear this conversation during tubby time with their preschool-aged children down the hall. So just to stop the bleeding, I dug into my pocket and came up with a couple of crinkled twenty-dollar bills, which I pressed into her sweaty white palm. The cash did the trick, but she flipped me the bird and belted out a final "FUCK YOU" as she wheeled around and stormed off toward the elevator.

When the coast was clear, I went back inside, closed the door, double-locked it, and fastened the chain for good measure. Now it was time to pay the piper.

"What was that all about?" Sari wanted to know.

"Eh . . . just a practical joke," I told her.

She wasn't amused and I got a tongue lashing. Hookers and Hampshire just don't mix.

9

GOING ONCE, GOING TWICE, GONE

IT WAS FEBRUARY 13, 1990, and I was a single man. I'd recently ended a long-term relationship, and I was looking to rebound. I accepted an invitation from the YWCA to take part in a charity bachelor auction. This meant that a bunch of female philanthropists would engage in a bidding war for a date with me. The proceeds would help rebuild the YWCA, so I saw it as a win-win.

The official rules for the auction, as printed in the program, were as follows:

1. A winning bid is a legal contract.
2. Bidding is limited to single or legally separated females who are at least twenty-one years of age.
3. The highest bidder will become purchaser of the date and must return to the cashier at the bidder's table for payment and to provide additional information immediately following a successful bid.

4. Winning bids are absolutely final. There will be no cancellations under any circumstances.

Each bachelor had to plan a date for himself and the lucky winner as part of the auction package. My date was dinner at Mickey Mantle's and a Knicks game. I wasn't sure how many bids this itinerary would draw amongst an erudite female crowd. I was hoping to attract someone athletic and down to earth. But I was up against some pretty stiff competition, such as the vice president of Bear Stearns, who offered a Broadway play of the lady's choosing followed by a helicopter tour of the city and a candlelit dinner at the Rainbow Room.

When I got up on the auction block with a long-stem rose in my mouth, I realized that the mob of 500-plus women was more interested in the bachelors themselves than the various dates they proposed. My date could have been a trip around the world on the *QE II* and it wouldn't have made me any more appealing. The ladies were looking for grade-A fresh meat.

Relishing the role reversal, the women howled and hooted their approval as I stepped forward in my tuxedo. My laid-back, low-octane date was the biggest cash cow of the evening, fetching $5,500 from the winning bidder.

Her name was Jody. She was short, with broad shoulders and lank, platinum blond hair with high school–style bangs. After the auction, she pulled me aside and introduced herself.

"Bill *Liederman*," she said. "Are you Jewish?"

"Yeah, why?"

"Well," she explained, "that means we can never get married. My parents would disown me."

"Well, that's okay," I said. "It's just a date."

"Yeah," she snorted, "one date for the low, low price of $5,500."

I felt like a piece of rump roast on the butcher's block.

"Do you want a refund?" I asked her. "I'm sure the next highest bidder would accept a date with a nice Jewish boy who still has all of his hair."

"No, I don't want a refund. But I don't want to go to Mickey Mantle's either. I don't want to sit there and get judged by each and every one of your employees."

"Okay . . . where would you like to go?"

"Any place else," she said, chugging a glass of champagne. "And forget the Knicks game. I'd rather have a leisurely dinner so we can get to know each other."

"And the Jewish thing?"

"Well," she mused, examining my profile, "you don't *look* Jewish. Maybe my parents will like you after all."

We agreed to meet the following Friday at Manhattan Market restaurant. On my way out the door, I was accosted by Denise Winston of Denise Winston Matchmaking Services. "Bill," she squealed, "I saw you up there, you looked great! You know, you would make a fabulous client for my firm. The membership fee is $5,000, but since you're such a great catch, I'll waive it for you."

She was like a scout at a high school basketball game, sniffing out the blue-chip prospects.

"I don't know, Denise," I said, gesturing back toward Jody. "I'm already hooked up with Ms. Fifty-Five Hundred."

"Not a chance," Denise chirped. "I've been in this business for twenty-five years, and I can tell right off the bat that you two are going nowhere."

When we met at Manhattan Market, the first order of business was to get shit-faced, so we downed three rounds of margaritas in the time it took for the appetizers to arrive. Of course, the drunker we got, the better she began to look.

We enjoyed some witty banter, none of which I remember because I was already wasting away in Margaritaville. After dinner, dessert, and cappuccino, the moment of truth arrived. When we hit a sobering blast of cold air on Second Avenue, I concluded it was time to say good night forever.

"Can I put you in a cab?" I asked her.

"No way," she yelled. "For $5,500, you are going to get into a cab with me and escort me home like the proper gentleman you say you are."

This didn't seem like too much to ask, but once we got inside the car, she scooted up next to me, closed her eyes, and tilted her head backward into the ready position for tonsil hockey.

I was starting to feel used. I held her off until the cab pulled up to her brownstone, at which point I helped her out of the cab and thanked her for a nice evening.

"For $5,500," she said, "the least you could do is walk me to the door and see me safely inside."

I really didn't want to, but I opted for the path of least resistance.

Once we got inside, she threw her arms around me and began dragging me into the bedroom.

"Look," I said, pulling away from her, "we had a really good time. Let's just leave it at that for tonight."

"What do you mean, leave it at that? For $5,500 I deserve a little more than just a peck on the cheek and a hug good night."

Apparently, Jody thought her $5,500 bid included a courtesy

fuck—as if that were included in the auction package. *Dinner at Mantle's and a Knicks game, followed by an all-night sex romp at your place!* With that kind of package, I could have fetched at least $5,501.

"I'm real tired," I explained, "and I'm just not that type of guy. Let's hook up again sometime and maybe we can get to know each other a little better."

"Bullshit," she cried, "you're never going to call me again!"

"Well, if that's your attitude, then maybe I won't."

"Fuck you," she said, and shoved me out onto the sidewalk. "This is the last time I'm going to waste my hard-earned money on some stupid bachelor auction."

I thought it a wise decision, but I remained mum.

Over the next few weeks, she called me several times, and once even threatened to call the YWCA and demand a complete refund for her total loser of a date.

Perhaps she should have called an escort service.

10

UNION BLUES

THE ORIGINAL PURPOSE of labor unions was to make sure employees earned a fair living wage with decent working conditions. Over the course of the last century, unions have saved many Americans from poverty, death, and despair. The labor movement has narrowed the gap between the haves and the have-nots, leading to the birth of a middle class. However, many of today's labor unions have perverted these principles beyond recognition, exerting a corruptive power over employers and employees alike.

In the food service industry, there are still some good unions, especially on the food-manufacturing and preparation end of the business. But for the most part, restaurant unions have traditionally been a boon only to the thugs, ex-cons, and bagmen who run them.

A few years back, my brother David and I signed a lease to open Television City, a television-themed restaurant, directly across the street from Radio City Music Hall, where Lindy's used to be. Lindy's was a Riese restaurant, along with Houlihan's, Friday's, and dozens of other dining establishments. When we signed our lease, the Rieses still had well over a year left on their lease. The Rieses agreed to vacate before their lease ran out but wanted to be partners in the new operation without investing a dime. We said no deal, so just to stick it to us, the Rieses held over for more than a year after their lease expiration date. Two hundred thousand dollars in legal fees later, they finally left under a court order, but not before destroying the infrastructure as a fare-thee-well gesture. They had their guys pouring cement down the drains and ripping apart the AC units on the roof. Talk about a welcome wagon. The scorched earth policy resulted in a five-and-a-half-million-dollar gut-renovation job and a grand opening three years behind schedule, at which time the theme restaurant boom had gone bust.

The design called for over a hundred theatrical stage lights, so we hired the same union that does the lighting for all the Broadway shows. At over a hundred dollars an hour, the rates were steep, but the guys put in a hard day's work and actually went the extra yard to get the job done right, sometimes staying to work late on their own time.

After a week of peace and prosperity with this particular union, a scar-faced hood named Vito meandered onto the job site. "I'm here to shut this job down," he threatened, spittle flying out from between his meaty lips.

Given his thuggish appearance, I decided against the standard quip, *Gimme the news, not the weather.* Telling him to *Say it, don't spray it* seemed equally inadvisable, so I simply asked, "What for?"

"Because you're running a nonunion job in a union location," he barked.

"No," I corrected him, "we're using a union."

I told him which one.

"That, my friend, is the wrong union," he said. "Either you switch to *our* union or I shut down the job. You've got twenty-four hours."

Somehow, after a lot of name-calling, we were able to reach an agreement allowing both unions to work the job. Vito's union would call all the shots. Three union electricians would work each ladder: a guy from the first union would hang the lights while one of Vito's guys steadied the base and another one handed up the tools. So, if anyone ever asks you how many union electricians it takes to screw in a lightbulb, the answer is three, at the combined cost of $500 an hour.

Vito's union worked slower and slower as our opening day deadline drew near. Now we were paying overtime to two different unions and the cost of screwing in bulbs rose to $750 an hour. Seven-hour workdays became four-hour workdays featuring coffee breaks—and soon that lightbulb was costing me $1,500 an hour to screw in. Bleeding cash like a stuck pig, I called for a sit-down with Vito.

"Look," I told him, "all I'm asking for is a fair day's work for a fair day's pay. Isn't that the union way?"

"Not ours," he said.

A few days later, when an enterprising rookie electrician of Vito's stepped up the pace, running circles around his somnolent coworkers, they retaliated by painting R-A-T on the site walls beneath unflattering drawings of his face on a rodent's body. He never came back to work.

Unions for restaurant employees are a different story altogether. Our local union had a death grip on hundreds of city eateries. Although that union did increase pay rates ever so slightly, the health benefits are shoddy at best, and the dues are so exorbitant. As a result, many back-of-house restaurant workers have learned to loathe the union. By and large, they prefer to work with independent restaurant owners. But many restaurants and hotels are stuck with unions and have to abide by the following rules: Chefs cannot actually cook anything, only supervise. Cooks cannot bake, and bakers cannot cook. Prep cooks can only do prep, like chopping onions, while dishwashers, who would give their dishwashing arms to do prep, are forbidden to do so. Dishwashers cannot mop the floors, so all mopping must be done by union porters. Any fissure in the ordained division of labor is reported to the union. Union establishments must hire a full crew of restaurant workers no matter how slow the business is, just to stand around and do nothing.

Dishwashers in big union hotels can make $75,000 a year with overtime. However, despite my own populist political leanings, it's impossible to operate nonunion joints like Mantle's under union stipulations, as payroll alone would be over 100 percent of the gross sales.

After three years of nonunion bliss at Mickey Mantle's, the staff seemed content. No dues, no silly workplace rules to follow, and plenty of scheduling flexibility. And then, when no one was looking, the unthinkable happened: a longtime waitress persuaded a third of her colleagues to sign a union questionnaire, thereby forcing an in-house election.

The entire staff received letters from the union stating that the restaurant belonged to the staff and not me. It was *their* restaurant, even though I was the one who had broken my balls to raise the money for construction with my personal guarantee on the line; their restaurant, even though they'd be gone as soon as they got a modeling gig or a better paying job. Their restaurant, indeed.

An election was scheduled for six months hence, and thus the campaign began. Union officials howled about working conditions and promised all manner of bennies and pay raises. Labor campaign rules prohibit restaurant management from promising these same things or meeting with employees one on one. Naturally, they also prohibit dismissal of any employee during this period, even if he or she is caught with her hand in the till. This gave the rogues amongst us several months to rip me off with absolutely no threat of managerial recourse.

At that time, Mantle's was grossing just north of four million a year, but due to occupancy costs, we were netting less than 2 percent. Union pay scales and health benefits were simply out of the question. Most porters made too much money to receive Medicaid and were too poor to pay for health insurance for themselves and their families. And this, my fellow Americans, is why our country needs a national health insurance policy.

We had to hire a powerful labor relations law firm and shell out a $25,000 retainer so they could advise us on how to win the election. We followed all NLRB rules according to Hoyle, as any misstep could result in an automatic union victory. Mickey threw his support behind me in fighting the union. His father, Mutt Mantle, had been a coal miner in the Oklahoma outback. As a kid, Mickey watched as his dad went on strike and the family sunk deeper into poverty. When the strike finally ended, Mutt went back to work for the same old wage, minus the cash he lost while he stood on the picket line. For this reason, Mick opposed the union, and I knew he had my back.

Other than that, I had no idea where I stood. I had about sixty employees eligible to vote, and there was no telling which way they would go. The day of the election, I was shitting a brick. If the union prevailed, Mantle's would evaporate under skyrocketing labor costs in a matter of months, and I would have to find a real job.

One by one, the employees made their way down to the cordoned-off dry-goods room to cast their votes. I searched their faces for some sign of predilection, but most of them gave me no clue. A union rep posted himself across from me, to be on the look-out for facial intimidation tactics.

When the final vote was cast, the union rep counted the ballots aloud, handing each one to me for inspection as he went along. Each ballot had two boxes on it: union yes and union no. The first one was a yes, and the next two were split. The next twenty-five after that were "union no," and the final tally was forty-eight to four, a landslide victory over the union.

Mickey and I celebrated, and before long, everything returned to normal. It was a lesson I couldn't have learned at Cornell's School of Industrial and Labor Relations.

11

SURVIVAL OF THE FITTEST

THE FAILURE RATE of new restaurants is said to be well over 90 percent. Every year when the Zagat guide comes out, I check the index to see which eateries have been toe-tagged. Many of them are yesterday's hot spots.

I always double-check to make sure Mantle's isn't one of them, like scanning the obits for your own death announcement.

People told me I was crazy for trying to open a sports bar on Central Park South. Most everyone I consulted with told me I would be doomed to immediate failure. I sifted through the negative feedback and decided to consult the most successful restaurateur I knew: Alan Stillman of Smith & Wollensky and the Park Avenue Café, among others. He'd broken into the restaurant major leagues as the original owner of the Friday's that later became the Manhattan Ocean Club at 58th Street between Fifth and Sixth avenues, a block south of the Mantle's construction site.

I called Stillman and asked him to stop by the location to check it out. On a honey of a spring day, he showed up, took a cursory look around, and said, "Bill, you are out of your mind. Only a madman would open a sports bar on Central Park South. That's like opening a McDonald's on the Champs Elysées."

"Let me explain," I assured him. "It's going to be an upscale sports bar, and . . ."

"No such thing," he interrupted. "No such category. No way."

He wished me luck ("You're going to need it—ha-ha!") and was off.

The only person who liked the location was Mickey himself, who knew nothing about restaurants except how to get drunk in them.

Many years later, Stillman opened the aptly named 1 CPS in the Plaza Hotel on the same block as Mickey Mantle's. The grand café served new American cuisine (small portions, high prices) for three years before going out of business. Nobody is sure what went wrong, but rumor has it that Eloise drove him out of business.

Meanwhile, the sports bar that Stillman condemned has outlasted almost every theme restaurant in the neighborhood, including Planet Hollywood, Motown Café, Harley-Davidson Café, the Fashion Café, and the Hard Rock Café. Dozens of little bistros from 55th to 58th streets have turned over in the last two decades. Italian places, Japanese, Indian, and Chinese. You name the country, it's had culinary representation in this neighborhood at some point or another. But it's easy come, easy go. Even my billionaire landlord couldn't hack it with Atlas, which he opened in his own building and essentially operated rent-free.

How has Mantle's survived for so many years? To what does the restaurant owe its longevity? There exist several theories—some plausible, some mystical, and some downright ridiculous. Here they are, in no particular order:

1. Mickey's legacy: When Mickey died in 1995, I figured that my run was just about over. But his folk-hero persona combined with the exalting press he received in his final battle with cancer actually increased business in the years since his passing.

2. Round-the-clock care: For almost as long as I owned Mickey Mantle's, I lived in the apartment building right above the store. Many restaurant failures result from absentee ownership.

3. Location, location, location: This explanation might apply, if all those other neighborhood eateries hadn't gone bye-bye. Our location wasn't too shabby, but it became a "destination location," meaning people didn't just happen by and stop in for lunch or dinner. The park was across the street, whereas a bustling office building would have afforded us more foot traffic.

4. Cheap rent—not: Mantle's opened on the heels of several failed restaurants in the same location. At the time, word on the street was that the spot was jinxed, a real consideration to many grizzled restaurant owners. Due to a lack of interest in the space, we got a pretty good deal going in: only $250,000 a year, or about $20,000 a month. Now, with those irksome little 2 percent annual rent increases over the last eighteen years, the annual occupancy cost, including rent, is now well over a million dollars per year. Not exactly rent-controlled housing. For perspective, take my former chef, Randy Pietro, the one with the seafood restaurant in Point Pleasant, New Jersey. His monthly rent is $1,250. Isn't that adorable?

And now, a word on real estate taxes: when Mayor "Money-bags" Bloomberg was elected, his first order of business was to raise real estate taxes by a whopping 18 percent. To many New Yorkers, this seemed like a decent move, as it balanced the budget and took a pound of flesh from greedy landlords and builders. However, in the case of mixed-use residential buildings with restaurants and retail shops, leases allow landlords to pass the buck, and the tax increases become the tenants' burden. This translated into a $100,000 annual occupancy increase for Mantle's. Many restaurants immediately collapsed under the weight of such increases.

Several years ago, public advocate Betsy Gotbaum came to Mantle's for lunch. I stopped by her table to chat her up, and after some small talk she asked me a question.

"Do you own this building?"

"No," I said, "I wish."

"Well, that's great, because the 18 percent tax increase won't affect you. What a marvelous piece of legislation for the mayor."

"Actually," I explained, "that's not how it works out. Most of the commercial leases contain clauses that allow landlords to pass tax increases along to the tenant. In our case, even though we occupy no more than 1 percent of the total space in this 300-unit apartment building, we have to swallow 10 percent of the increase. In many buildings, landlords have legally allocated well over 100 percent of the increase to their commercial tenants."

Betsy was incredulous.

"That's got to be illegal," she surmised.

"Actually, no," I informed her. "There are no laws about over-allocating. Whatever the lease says, goes."

"Wow," she said, "I learn something new every day. If I had known that the bulk of the increase fell on tenants like you, I would never have supported the legislation."

"That's okay," I said. "You didn't know."

"Now I do," she said, "and after lunch, I'm going to bring this to the mayor's attention."

Perhaps most important to the restaurant's runaway success was Mickey's unending love for the place.

"Bill," he said to me on more than one occasion, "promise me that when I'm dead and gone, this place will still be here for the fans. If it wasn't for them, I'd be nothing."

The words may sound trite, but they were his.

12

BOTTOMS UP

DURING THE HOLIDAY season, restaurants often toss their employees a few crumbs: featuring over-the-hill, off-the-menu bottles of wine, goodies extorted from the bar snacks guy, teas from the tillerman, and anything else that can be strong-armed from the butcher, the baker, or the candlestick maker.

A simple *Look motherfucker, either you come up with fifty fruit cakes for the staff, or we delete you from our purveyor list* usually does the trick. At Mantle's, we wailed away at our apparel guy, Phil Livoti of Apsco, for free Christmas gifts. By providing the entire staff with free Mickey Mantle's backpacks, Phil knew he was securing his place as our exclusive T-shirt purveyor for the coming year, and thus, he went for it every time. Then he'd tweak his prices over the course of that year in order to cover his cost for the free gifts.

Another perk bestowed on restaurant employees is the notorious holiday staff party. Timing for this event is crucial. If you throw it too early in December, you can't threaten to call it off for lackluster service during the Christmas rush. The middle to the end of December is no good either, because the staff will get soused and call in sick for one of the busiest days of the season. The best time to throw the bash is during the first week of January, right before business falls off a cliff and layoffs begin.

Food cost for a staff Christmas party is less than 1 percent of nothing. Between the leftovers in the walk-in box and whatever free food you can leverage out of the purveyors, the feast is on, big time. The same goes for the booze. Liquor purveyors would much rather toss you a full bar for free than lose your account or have their premium brands dropped from the restaurant's top shelf. Bottoms up.

Since the booze is free, staff members forgo the old adage of "never mix, never sorry" and sample some of everything at the bar: champagne, scotch, Jägermeister, Grey Goose, Herradura, and Johnny Walker Red, Black, and blue, to name a few. As the evening wears on, blood alcohol levels skyrocket and the dancing and flirting give way to groping and projectile vomiting. At the end of each annual fete, I would walk somberly throughout the restaurant, surveying the carnage like King Arthur on the battlefields: a waitress passed out with her head in the toilet, a busboy sleeping soundly in the laundry basket under a pile of dirty napkins, a cook lying comatose on the prep table with a string of drool dangling from his slack mouth onto the cold, tile floor—and on and on, ad nauseam.

The Christmas party is a very colorful event, as it merges the two different camps of restaurant staff. Cooks are from Uranus and servers are from Venus. Under normal circumstances, the back-of-house boys don't get to mingle with the front-of-house waitresses and hostesses. The ladies are all aspiring starlets, and a dishwasher from Honduras has about a zero percent chance of scoring with the next Julia Roberts. But booze equals bravado, so the staff party is a carnivalesque exception to the rule. The amigos get loaded and whip out their best pickup lines, albeit in broken English.

All year long, the waitresses have been prancing past the cook line on their way to the locker rooms and back, shaking their booties and flipping their hair to taunt the sweaty cooks. At the Christmas party, the ladies slip into their Saturday night best and get lit up like bonfires. The two camps usually spend the first hour of the shindig in their separate corners before starting to mix. Given that white men can't dance, the Latinos own the dance floor, luring the objects of their fancy into a sexy salsa scenario. These guys can really dance, and given that many of the waitresses are song 'n' dance gals anyway, they become a perfect fit as dancing partners. Before long, our dishwashing lothario begins to believe he may end up in bed with the princess/waitress.

Of course, the girls just wanna have fun and have absolutely no intention of doing anything more than dirty dancing. But the macho-men and the fallout can be downright ugly. Starting the very next shift, the cock-teasing waitresses are subjected to delayed food orders, making it impossible for them to serve their tables on time. In the wake of all the dirty dancing, sexual harassment in the kitchen rises to depcom 3.

One year, John, an inked-up, Trans Am–driving prep cook from Bay Ridge, hooked up with Daisy, a wafer-thin, Midwestern waitress with a recurring nonspeaking role on *Days of Our Lives*. After dancing provocatively for over an hour, the two of them mysteriously disappeared.

Before we could round up a posse, the case was cracked. Behind a column in the main dining room, standing up, John had mounted Daisy from the rear and was totally fucking her. What the future porn stars didn't know was that a large mirror adjacent to the column was beaming their XXX-rated act to all the holiday revelers.

With a brazenness only binge drinking can buy, the entire staff drained from the dance floor and bum-rushed the happy humpers, forming a peanut gallery six-deep around the scene of the crime.

"Lets go John-ny! Let's go John-ny," they chanted in unison, clapping and stamping their feet like a bunch of rednecks at a hoedown.

John and Daisy were so wasted they didn't seem to mind. They threw on their clothes and left the party.

The next day, Mantle's was abuzz with John and Daisy's remake of *Love Story*. Love may mean "never having to say you're sorry," but the two of them were so sorry they never set foot in the place again, not even to collect their paychecks.

13

THE BENGALI BUTTERBALL

In eighteen years at Mantle's, I have employed hundreds of people. The cooks and porters are almost all lifers, so turnover in that department is front-page news. The service staff has a much larger turnover, as waiters and bartenders chase their dreams of acting, and, in a few dream-come-true scenarios, go on to successful show-biz careers. So far we have had Jamie Karen, the second female lead in *Man of La Mancha,* the male lead in a series of Staples commercials, a Nets dancer, a CBGB's rocker, a buzz-worthy stand-up comedienne named Becky Donohue, and a few nurses and maids in various soap operas.

To this day, only one original staff member remains, like a dung beetle after the A-bomb dropped on the Japs. The guy talks faster than even I do, which I'm told is almost impossible to do. Then there's the accent: a thick Bengali babble, punctuated by an anemic attempt to mimic mainstream American English. If you close your eyes he sounds like Elmer Fudd on crystal meth.

He showed up at the site every day until the restaurant was opened, clad in a shiny zoot suit and pleading incoherently for a job.

I had a position for a busser open, and it seemed easier to hire him than to send him away again, only to have him back the next day.

Within three years, he had worked his way up to runner, and somewhere around the summer of 1998, I succumbed to his lobbying and made him a waiter. My managers thought I was nuts to stuff him into a baseball jersey and sic him on actual paying customers.

Eighteen years later, Mo can still be heard reciting the dessert menu to bewildered customers: "We hab fibe gwate dessuh: de boobewwy cobwah, da shockwit shunk wice poodin', de New Yuck sheeshkick, de shawbewwy shootcake, and de hot pudge boonie sundae. Whachoo like?"

Somehow, despite his indecipherable pitch, he always leads the league in dessert sales and overall check average. I think sometimes people order dessert just to get him to shut his mouth.

In addition to his linguistic shortcomings, his behavior has always been a bit spastic and off-kilter. Don't get me wrong: he's got a good heart, and he's matured enough over the years to have made lasting workplace friendships. But he's nosy, he's abrasive, he's unabashedly greedy, and he laughs loudly (before the punch line) at jokes he doesn't understand. Then he usually reciprocates by telling a little joke of his own. He has about a half-dozen of them in his comic arsenal. Here's an oldie-but-goodie: "Pantyhose, m' wife. I seh, why you no wear? Why no pen-hose? She say, 'Nooooo, my don't like.' I say, 'Fy, no pwobem . . . no like, no wear!' That's it. HAHAHA."

Don't get it? How about this one: "Bengaladesh, I go fishmawket. See niiiiiice piece, a boo-full fish. Niiiiice. Nice scales. BIG! I say, 'How musha wan, dis fish?' Man say, 'Dis biiiiig fish. Dis fwesh.' He name pwice, little mo den twelve dollah, Amewica dollah. I say, 'No sir, I gib ten dollah, whole fish.' He say, 'No way

. . .' I say, 'No fish!' Walk away. HAHAHA. I buy uddah fish, cheap. My wife make . . . oils, wedge-tables, gah-lic, nice!"

Mo was but a squishy, single-browed man-child with a penchant for ratting out his colleagues in order to make himself look more important. His parents had owned a restaurant of their own in Bangladesh, which made him think he knew better than everybody else—a belief that he was quick to point out to those around him. To say the least, his arrogance didn't fly with his coworkers, and his linguistic shortcomings (combined with his resemblance to Humpty-Dumpty) made him a target of torture for every joke. Among an all-Latino kitchen staff, he stuck out like a jumbo platter of Tandoori chicken.

As a runner, he spent a great deal of time going mano-a-mano with the kitchen crew. On a nightly basis, there was what came to be known as the "Mohammed flare-up," which often led to a shoving match between Mo and whoever was fed up with him.

On one such evening, he tangled with Kenny, a fellow runner and a tough-talking Puerto Rican macho-man from East Harlem. A solid six foot two and 215 pounds of pure muscle-bound madness, Kenny was exactly the type of guy you don't want to meet in a dark alley, or in the employee washroom, for that matter. The fight flared up over which table a particular plate of ribs was going to, and they began a shoving match that resulted in the ribs being dumped on the floor.

"Te voy a matar, gordo hijo de puta," Kenny bellowed above the peals of laughter from the cook line. "Te voy facar el corozon del pecho y me voy cagar en el!"

Foolhardy as ever, and without the slightest clue as to what had just been said to him, Mo fired back in riddled English, "I gonna keek you fuggin' butt, mudder-fugger. You weel pay, son of piss!"

I doubt Kenny had ever been called such a name, so you had to give Mo points for originality. Nobody in the kitchen lifted a pinky to break up the fight, even as Kenny grasped Mo by his shirt collar and wrung his paunchy frame clear off the ground. They all wanted to see—would have *paid* to see—their homeboy kick the shit out of "that fat Indian prick," as they called him in casual conversation. Mo loathed being referred to as Indian and preferred to be called Bengali, his actual heritage. "Dere is diffwance," he always insisted. But what that difference was, the amigos didn't know and didn't care.

As Kenny raised Mo's pudgy visage to meet his snarl, Mo poked Kenny in both eyes, Three Stooges–style. Kenny, caught totally off guard, flung Mo against the salad station and seized a ten-inch carving knife from behind the grill and lunged at the doughboy like a slasher in a B horror flick. A couple of cooks jumped out from behind the line and tied up his arms just before the knife was lost forever in Mohammed's bulging gut.

Mo hauled ass to the manager on duty and lodged a complaint, which she relayed to me first thing the next morning. As a rule, I never believe anything unless I see it, so I knew it was time to summon the two would-be warriors to a powwow in my underground lair.

Before rounding them up, I met with the two men individually. Mo was a perennial troublemaker and a constant source of aggravation. Kenny was a solid employee who had the respect of every prep cook and dishwasher in his domain. In the ongoing war between the front and the back of the house that is waged in every restaurant the world over, Kenny was a valuable liaison between opposing sides. Despite what I'd heard of his aggressive indulgence, I wanted to keep him on staff. I called him in first, alone, and asked for his side of the story.

I knew Kenny was supporting a family of five, so as he appeared in the office and took the seat across from me, I expected him to take one of the following three routes: (a) deny that a knife was involved, (b) say he was only kidding, (c) apologize profusely. And then there was (d): none of the above.

He went for (d).

"Kenny," I asked him, "Did you pull a knife on Mohammed last night?"

"FUCK, YEAH," he roared, puffing out his mammoth pecs.

"Why?"

"Because," he explained, "I wanted to kill that fat Indian motherfucker."

This was not the answer I was looking for, and sadly, I had to let him go. He understood this to be his fate. His truthful statement about the incident during our brief meeting of the minds had been a conscious choice. I think underneath it all, Kenny was afraid of spending the rest of his life at Shawshank for stuffing Mo into the incinerator.

On his way out of the office, Kenny made a final run at Mohammed, who had his ear to the door the whole time. Somehow, Mo wriggled out of Kenny's grasp and made for the meat freezer, where he remained inside, hiding until the coast was clear.

Upstairs, Kenny made a final lap through the kitchen, getting a hero's farewell along with pounds and high fives, as if he had hit a walk-off game 7 World Series home run.

Several years ago Mo played the role of groom in a traditional Bengali arranged wedding. When he came back to work after a month's absence, he was quick to show off his wedding photos. She wore traditional, multi-colored Bengali vines and her gorgeous face (picture a Bengali Denise Richards) was twisted into what looked like a permanent scowl. In all their snapshots, Mo beams with pride and glee—oblivious to her absolute misery.

Rumor has it that she went out and bought a size 32 belt and announced that she would not be coming to America until the belt fit. Unfortunately, a 44 doesn't fit into a 32.

The grapevine says that Mo is still toiling at Mantle's and is about to have a child with his arranged wife. Mo is a first ballot inductee into my restaurant Hall of Fame.

He is truly a sweetheart and a big-hearted guy and the top-earning server at Mantle's. If you stop into Mickey's, tell him I sent you. He will take good care of you.

14

MIKE THE COP

OFFICER MIKE is right out of a Norman Rockwell painting. He's the friendliest cop on the beat. There he is, standing in front of the barbershop, giving a lollipop to the towheaded eight-year-old boy. He's the best friend and big-brother figure for everyone in the small town of Mayberry. He evokes images of other cops we knew as children, before the notion of rogue cops was introduced by movies and television shows such as *Serpico, The French Connection,* and *Hill Street Blues.* It wasn't until my high school days— when, during the Vietnam War protests, I joined the chants of "off the pig"—that a cop was anything other to me than a blue knight in shining armor.

When Mantle's opened in 1988, a cop in his third year of service pulled up in front of the restaurant in one of those itty-bitty, three-wheel scooters, which fit his six-foot-one, 290-pound frame like a Playtex living car with four large boxes of Dunkin' Donuts riding shotgun. This is when I first met Officer Mike. A former all-city guard with Archbishop Molloy High School, he'd averaged 18.3 points a game and won a full boat with St. John's. Mike was unable to compete at this level and lasted only one season, which he spent riding the pines.

Mike the Cop squeezed himself out of his ridiculous little buggy and eased through the revolving doors at Mantle's. I stepped forward to greet him.

"Hey," he said, "I'm Mike, the cop on the beat."

"Great," I replied, "welcome to Mickey's. Where's the rest of your beat?"

"Pretty much just this block and wherevah," he said, waving his arms around like a whirlybird. "Anytime you need me, you can pretty much find me hanging out front in my scootah."

We shot the shit for a few minutes, and then Mike hunkered down in the back room of Mickey's to do police work, which consisted of guzzling coffee and snarfing donuts. Before long his walkie-talkie began to sputter with activity.

"We have a four-oh-one-niner in section eight at 22 West 56th Street. Please respond."

"What's a four-oh-one-niner?" I couldn't help but ask.

"Ah, nothin'. Just an armed robbery a couple of blocks away," he explained, switching off his radio with a decisive snap.

"Why'd you turn it off?" I wanted to know.

"I've heard enough of that crap for one day."

"But don't you have to go to the scene of the crime?"

"Nah, I don't wanna get hurt. Let the other guys in Midtown North respond to that one."

Recently, after twenty years of service, Mike hung up his badge and enjoys half pay with full medical insurance plus twelve grand a year from the City of New York for the rest of his life. (All the cops like Mike try to pile up overtime during their last year on the force because the half payment they will receive forever is based on their gross income for the last twelve months.) Not too shabby for a healthy man of forty-five. He always dreamed of moonlighting at Mickey's, drinking Coronas while keeping the bar free of pickpockets and ruffians. Maybe you can find him there.

It turns out that Mike's duties include far more than just cruising the beat in his mini-mobile and holding court at Mantle's. On the contrary, he has a hodgepodge of different tasks, all worthy of battle pay.

1. Security: Many mornings he could be found on duty at Rockefeller Center overseeing the early a.m. rock and roll show. Of course, this didn't affect his duties on the Mickey's beat because by the time we opened at 11:00 a.m., the telecast was long over.

2. Funeral duty: Several days a week, he was an honor guard at the funerals of police officers. This took about three hours from start to finish and gave him the rest of the day off because of union rules.

3. The athletic component: He played on the Midtown North softball and basketball teams. Mike is an all-star third sacker and almost never booted the ball. If he misjudged one, he let it bounce off his Kevlar vest, picked it up, and fired a heat-seeking missile to first base. He was also one of the best hitters in the league. Best of all, his game was never affected by one too many brewskies. In fact, he performed better with a full load on.

4. Social coordination, including frequent lunch meetings at Mantle's with other members of the force: Every few weeks, he brought in a motley menagerie of cops, including Stew the Jew, Charlie the Chink, Flynn the Mick, and Dick the

Dago—as they whimsically referred to one another. They would sit around and discuss police business, such as where they were going to get wasted that evening and what they were going to do when their twenty years ran out. These meetings usually lasted about two hours or so. The cops drowned their sorrows in diet colas and iced teas until quittin' time, and then it was on to the big-boy beverages.

Speaking of drinking, it's interesting to note that cops can drink like fish and nobody seems to care. It kind of goes with the territory. However, if they test positive for one bong hit, they are thrown off the force—no pension, no benefits, no questions asked. The message: fellow officers, go ahead and drink yourselves to death, but don't you dare touch that evil weed. Mike, a former teenage pothead, has a recurring post-retirement dream: he rolls a fat joint the size of a Cuban cigar and smokes the whole thing himself. Irie, man. Irie!

Mike's resumé at Midtown North contains a small flurry of parking tickets and no arrests whatsoever. When I probed him about the absence of collars, he answered without hesitation: "Are you fucking kidding me? If I collar a skell, I have to go to court and do a shit-load of paperwork. Who the fuck needs that?"

Once I asked him if he would ever take a detectives test or go for captain.

"For what?" he scoffed. "So I can get myself killed?"

Another time I asked him how he got such a cushy assignment.

"I got a rabbi," was all he said. He wouldn't elaborate.

Over the years, Mike and I have become best buddies. He's spent more time protecting Mantle's than being at home with his brave wife. We've laughed together, drank together, and rubbed elbows with Mickey and all the other high-profile jocks at Mantle's together. He was a keynote speaker at my fiftieth birthday roast, where he forgot all the lines that I had written for him and proceeded to mumble some shit that nobody understood. But I let him slide on stuff like that, because it's nice to have the extra measure of free security around at all times.

I believe it is because of this extra protection that Mantle's has never suffered a serious robbery. We've seen our share of pickpockets and barroom brawls, but, minor skirmishes not withstanding, Mantle's might just be the safest place on the planet. I mean, shit . . . some people get a pet Doberman for protection; we've got a pet cop.

Best of all, Mike is a really good sport. I could count on his unflinching participation in all of my practical jokes that required uniformed police officers.

I had a neighbor named Kurt who lived a few floors below me at 40 Central Park South. Kurt was a good-natured guy with a few garden-variety personal problems: cocaine addiction, alcoholism, compulsive lying, and compulsive gambling. But because we were neighbors, bachelors, and big sports fans, Kurt and I hung out a little bit, during which time he tried to stick some of his cocaine-fueled delusional business deals on me. On several occasions, he hooked me into projects that resulted in a sea of red ink covered over by a metric ton of outrageous lies. It was time for Kurt to pay the piper.

Kurt had mentioned to me that his most important client would be lunching with him at Mickey's, and would I please stop over to the table to make him look good? Game on!

I enlisted Officer Mike, who was hanging out at the bar, talking shit with a couple of regulars. We huddled up and I drew out the play with Xs and Os on a bar-nap. Mike asked me to go over the play a few more times, and I obliged him, until my scheme was firmly lodged in his thick Irish skull.

When Kurt arrived, I made sure that he and his guest were seated at a table, in plain view, smack down in the middle of the dining room. After their lunch arrived, I gave Mike the thumbs up and he lumbered on over to the table, dutiful as a Labrador retriever.

"Excuse me, sir. Is your name Kurt?" he asked, deadpan and determined.

"Why yes I am," Kurt replied uneasily. "What can I do for you, officer?"

Without a moment's hesitation, Mike whipped out his unused ten-year handcuffs and held them up high to make sure everyone in the restaurant was watching, then gave them a hearty jangle before cuffing Kurt's arms to the chair.

"Kurt Carlson," he proclaimed, "you are under arrest for withholding child support."

I tried not to burst out howling as the color drained from Kurt's face. He had never been married and, as far as he knew, he had no children.

"You have the right to remain silent. Anything you say can and will be used against you in a court of law. You have the right to an attorney. If you cannot afford one, one will be provided to you by the State of New York. Do you understand these rights as I have explained them to you?"

"*No*," Kurt squealed. "What child support? I don't have any children!"

"Yeah, yeah. That's what all the perps say," Mike growled. "Our records show that you have three different kids with three different women in three different states."

It was then that Kurt's extra-special client excused himself and made for the door.

"Oh, come on," Kurt blubbered, "this is a huge mistake. I didn't do anything wrong and I want to talk to my lawyer."

"You can call your lawyer from the station house. Of course, we could just skip central booking for an immediate payment of $10,000 to be distributed among your three wives."

"What?"

"You heard me," Mike grumbled. "Just write me a check or it's off to the lockup with your deadbeat dad ass."

Kurt was fumbling for his checkbook, and when Mike let him in on the joke, I popped out from behind a column, the two of us howling like jackals. Kurt, on the other hand, was not amused.

"Fuck you, Liederman," he snarled. "Your ass is grass!"

Mike took his sweet time locating the appropriate key. No sooner had the lock clicked open than Kurt burst out of his chair and stormed upstairs to his apartment, no doubt to load his nose.

"Hey Kurt," I called after him between peals of laughter. "Payback's a bitch!"

By the end of that year, Kurt had welched on several more promises and refused to pay me some money he lost to me betting pro basketball, and it was time to remind him what we do to bullshit artists at Mantle's. So, once again, I recruited Mike the Cop. "But, Bill, you cock-knocker," he objected, "it'll never work. He already knows what I look like."

"No matter," I said, drawing up the new plan on a fresh napkin. "I got me an idea."

I explained to Mike that Kurt had this really cute dog, a spotted pointer named Pippin, after the Chicago Bull great. Kurt worshipped this precious pooch, especially since his latest girlfriend had moved out. The next day at lunch, Kurt sat at Mickey's favorite booth, with three important marks (I mean potential clients). As soon as they'd all hunkered down, Officer Mike cupped his hands around his mouth and broadcast an announcement: "Does anyone here own a brown-and-white pointer spaniel by the name of Pippin?"

Kurt sprang to his feet, wide-eyed.

"Yeah, right here . . . that's my dog! That's my boy. That's my buddy boy. That's my buddy boy baby."

"Well, I'm sorry to inform you that your dog has just been hit by a double-decker bus in front of the restaurant."

"Oh, NO," Kurt wailed. "Not my Pippin, not my Pippin! *Nooo!*" You'd think he had lost his entire family in a fiery wreck.

Meanwhile, I had used a passkey to get into Kurt's crib and was holding Pippin in the bathroom. I waited a few dozen delicious seconds before releasing the hound, who bounded over to the table and leaped into his master's lap.

"Oh, thank God, Pippin; I thought I had lost you," Kurt moaned, pelting the pooch with frantic kisses. "Oh, thank God, Pippin. You're alive; you're *aliiiiiive!*"

When he had finished rejoicing, he turned his attention to me.

"You cocksuckers! I'm going to get you if it's the last thing I ever goddamn do! C'mon, Pippin, let's go."

A few years ago, we had a problem with the management of the St. Moritz Hotel, now the Ritz-Carlton, which is located wall to wall with Mickey's. Ian Schrager, the famed Studio 54 felon and boutique restaurant impresario, had bought the hotel and planned to convert it into a trendy minimalist flophouse. After moving in, Schrager's first order of business was to shroud the entire block with oppressive scaffolding, burying Mantle's in a forest of iron crossbars and blue plywood.

I asked Schrager if he would mind if I attached a Mickey Mantle's banner to the scaffolding so that people could actually find my front door. He refused, claiming that a sign would interfere with the minimalist look he was trying to cultivate.

I called for backup. Mike the Cop arrived on his scooter in under five minutes, and we drew up a quick game plan: every car, limo, taxi, and the like that pulled up in front of the St. Moritz would be ticketed, even if they were still moving. Officer Mike and his crew dropped over a hundred tickets that day, one on any vehicle that dared to roll up to the hotel.

Schrager figured it all out in no time flat. The next day, I got a call from one of his goons. "Mr. Schrager asked me to tell you that he would be delighted if you would hang a Mickey Mantle's sign up on the scaffolding."

"Thanks a million," I replied, chuckling to myself.

We never had another problem with the hotel.

As Mike's time on the force dwindled, I began to mess with his head even more often. Every time he left his scooter unattended, I loaded up the windshield wipers with various foodstuffs. Turkey burgers, hoagie rolls, tomato slices, and big, floppy lettuce leaves. Sometimes I even sprung for a box of donuts. The first time I did it, Mike was still bleary-eyed from a night of fighting for truth, justice, and the American way at a local cop watering hole, and he was way too blitzed to notice. He actually pulled up to the Midtown

North station house with a bacon, lettuce, and tomato sandwich plastered to his windshield. All the cops at the station noticed, and for a few minutes he was the laughingstock of New York's Finest. Mike wasted no time getting me on the phone.

"You cock-knocker," he howled. "I'm going to kick your ass!"

"What's the matter, Mike?" I replied. "Did you say hold the mayo?"

15

CELEBRITY PROFILES

WHEN IT COMES TO celebrity clientele, who's naughty and who's nice? Here are my picks—from the good to the bad to the ugly.

Tricky Trump

By 1991, it was common knowledge that Donald Trump, who was married to Ivana at the time, had become friendly with model/fledgling actress Marla Maples. Furthermore, it was also common knowledge around Central Park South that he was stashing the starlet in the St. Moritz.

One night, he picked her up at the hotel and the two of them escaped next door to Mickey's for a burger. At the time, Trump was at the top of his game building casinos in Atlantic City. He was "The Prince of the City," and despite his comb-over hairdo and sallow complexion, his charisma was of a rare ilk: something akin to Mickey's or even JFK's. Everyday people just wanted to touch him in the hopes that some of his money and power would rub off on them.

If Marla Maples were a piece of clothing, she'd be a fluffy pink angora sweater. Some said she had taken over for Little Richard as the new Georgia Peach. She had one of those perfect-body-meets-perfect-smile-meets-perfect-blond-hair looks working for her. Above all, she was a classic girly-girl, and in her warm brown eyes, there was a cheerleader-like innocence and warm enthusiasm that could melt an iceberg.

Together, they made a compelling couple as they sat there nibbling on their burgers. Other customers watched from a distance, fearful of disrupting some important conversation about Donald's impending divorce.

Somewhere between burgers and dessert, Trump waved me over for a tableside chat. Trying to seem as debonair as humanly possible, I sauntered coolly to his booth thinking I'd say something witty, like, *Perhaps you'd like to buy this restaurant for thirty million dollars!*

But when I got there, all I could muster was, "Welcome to Mickey's, Mr. Trump."

"How's business?" he asked me, taking a dainty sip of his Diet Coke.

"Great," I replied. "We've been open three years, and I've paid my investors back every penny they invested."

I was angling for the thirty mil, hoping to impress him with my investor track record.

"Now, Bill," he asked in mock bewilderment, "why the hell would you ever want to pay your investors back?" Trump threw his head back and roared with laughter, his hairdo retaining an uncanny stasis.

The conversation was over. I slunk away, marveling at Marla's magnificence.

The next year, I accompanied Mickey to the '61 New York Yankees reunion show at Trump's Taj Mahal casino in Atlantic City. I bumped into Ritchie Rich once during a photograph session and muttered something about the time we met at Mickey's. Not recognizing me in the slightest, he said, "Sure, I remember," and slithered past me to talk to someone else.

After the show, I flew Trump's helicopter service back to New York by myself, as Mickey was continuing south to Washington, D.C., to appear at an autograph show. By the time I was seated and the whirlybird was ready to take off, there was just one open seat, and that one seat just happened to be the window seat next to mine.

I was hoping that a big, smelly casino-loser wouldn't plop himself down next to me. Instead, I got Donald Trump. As he took his seat and buckled up, I reintroduced myself, and we got to chatting. I could not believe my luck; I had a forty-minute locked-in audience with the world's richest man.

As the helicopter lifted off the launching pad next to the Taj, Trump pointed down to a humongous piece of vacant property on the boardwalk, connected to the Taj by a covered footbridge.

"I own all that, too," he bragged, then popped the question: "How would you like to open a Mickey Mantle's on the pier right across from the Taj?"

"Sure," I said casually, donning my game face. "But who's gonna pay for the build-out? I'm just a single-unit guy, and . . ."

"No, no, no," Trump interjected, "I'll build it. I'll pay for everything, and we'll do a joint venture."

After a career of eking out a living, I had hit the lottery! Trump went on to explain that his top real estate lieutenant, Mr. Mark Merken, would contact me to "do the deal."

"It'll be real smooth," he added, making that *real-smooth* hand gesture with his down-turned palm. "It's an easy deal to make. Mickey's would do great in Atlantic City. A real win-win for both of us." Having said his piece, he turned to the window and gazed out at all that he owned. The great and powerful Oz had spoken.

The next day, as Trump had promised, Merken called. We arranged a lunch meeting to go over the particulars. When he arrived, I was taken aback by his formidable presence. A former University of North Carolina basketball player under Dean Smith, he was six foot seven and weighed about 280. His massive hands were like sledgehammers, pounding the table to emphasize his deal points.

"The rent," he explained, "is fifty thousand dollars a month. Donald will need a six-month security deposit. Donald will also need to approve your architect and contractor. You gotta figure you're going to spend about two hundred and fifty dollars per square foot to build it."

"Wait a minute," I countered, "Mr. Trump said he was going to pay for the build-out."

"Don't be silly," Merken scoffed, "Donald Trump doesn't pay for anything."

"But . . . Mr. Trump said we were going to be partners on this."

"You must have misunderstood," Merken retorted. "The last thing Donald needs is another partner. You've gotta pay for your own build-out. That's the deal, take it or leave it."

I left it, and he left.

Postscript: The All-Star Café ended up opening in that space, and it promptly went bankrupt.

Ragin' Reggie

By a long shot, the biggest asshole ever to darken my restaurant door is Reginald Martinez Jackson. When the restaurant first opened, Reggie stopped by to gift us with an autographed photo to adorn our wall. It was a classic shot of Reggie's home run swing, the one where his left knee seems to be touching the turf in the batter's box. Better yet, it was inscribed: *To Mickey, the greatest of all time. Best wishes, Reggie Jackson, #44.*

After thanking him for the generous gift, I asked him if he wanted a tour. He said no, he's gotta run—but the next time he's in, would I please show him where I'd hung the picture?

He returned later that season. Hoping this might be the beginning of a beautiful relationship with the Yankee slugger, I greeted him warmly, but his eyes were stormy and foreboding. If his countenance was a weather report, it would have forecasted a 100 percent chance of a shit storm.

"Hey, Reggie," I said gingerly, "wanna see where I hung your picture?"

"Fuck OFF," he snarled, turning on his heel like a Pamplona bull and spinning out the door like a Pamplona bull.

Several years later, Major League Baseball threw a "Heroes of the Game" contest to inaugurate the Rangers new stadium in Arlington, Texas. The game was sponsored by Upper Deck, the memorabilia company that had just signed Mickey to a multiyear, multimillion-dollar autograph contract. Mickey was invited, of course, and because Arlington is near his Dallas residence, he accepted and invited me and a date to join him in the dugout during the game.

When I arrived with Hampshire Sari, we were ushered to our seats in the dugout, which Mickey had arranged for us, and watched the delicious sight of Hall of Famers going about the business of being baseball heroes when I noticed two things: not only was the recently retired Reggie sitting alone, but all the other ballplayers were going out of their way to avoid him. Every time he tried to approach the Hall of Famers, they scattered. It seemed that only Mickey would acknowledge him. Mick shot the shit with him briefly, but before too long he pulled himself away and wandered off to go mingle with his good old guys.

Reggie suddenly spun around, catching Sari and me in his nasty glare. Flaring his nostrils like an enraged bull, he bounded down the dugout steps to greet us warmly.

"What the fuck are you two doing in the dugout?"

I said, "Mickey invited us."

Reggie said, "Horseshit."

I said, "Ask Mickey," to which he replied, "FUCK OFF," before storming back over to Mickey.

By this point they were out of earshot, but we could see what was happening. Reggie pointed at us with a meaty digit, and Mickey nodded his head in the affirmative. But Reggie wasn't done raging, and once Mickey turned away, he skipped back on down the dugout steps for round two.

"Okay," he conceded, "so you're here with Mick. But if you're going to sit on that bench, sit at the end of it, away from the players."

"Yeah, fine," I answered, and we scooted on down to the very end of the bench.

In the next inning, Reggie went to bat praying for a tater, but he grounded out to first. He cursed and punched the air like some sort of overgrown man-baby having a tantrum. Struggling to lend adequate expression to his rage, he ripped off his batting helmet and hurled it into the dugout.

Spying me and Sari on the bench, he ran at us with his lips peeled back like a bloodthirsty Doberman, ready for the third and final round.

"YOU FUCKERS," he roared, "I thought I told you to MOVE OVER."

"Yeah," I agreed, "and we did. And here we are."

"MORE," he roared, gesturing wildly, even though we were already up against the wall.

Sari edged into my lap, and somehow we managed to exile ourselves even more. By this point, we were pressed up against the wall at the far end of the dugout like we were trying to burrow a hole through to the other side. Finally, Mickey turned around and caught a glimpse of the madness.

"Leave them alone," he drawled. "I told you they're mah goddamn fray-unds."

Thus ended Reggie's raging—for the time being. His ego called for a monster tater in the new stadium, but his creaking body yielded only four slow rollers out to first base, much to the Hall of Famers' unanimous delight.

A final note on Ragin' Reggie: A couple of years ago, I was walking down Sixth Avenue, around the corner from Mickey's, when along came Reggie Jackson from the opposite direction. Not looking up, he expectorated, shooting a major-league loogie from his mouth like a daredevil out of a circus cannon. The giant phlegm ball barreled at me, missing my face by around four inches. Even though I've never been in a fight, if that scud missile had connected, I would have kicked the shit out of him. Someday, somebody will.

Almighty Ali

I had three childhood heroes: Mickey Mantle, Muhammad Ali, and Bill Bradley. I grew up in Princeton, New Jersey, and as a junior high school student, I had the privilege of attending all of Dollar Bill's college basketball games. I was sitting on the floor under the basket when—as a *freshman*—he made his record fifty-seventh straight foul shot.

The Greatest has visited Mantle's on several occasions, the last of which was in 2001. My one-and-a-half-year-old baby Emmy was with me that evening. When Ali saw Emmy, he picked her up and tried to plant a smooch on her pudgy face. Wise beyond her years, she refused his advance, snapping her head sideways as if she were slipping a left jab, then going on the attack with a right slap-jab of her own. Ali absorbed the blow, feigning an effort to stay on his feet before collapsing on the floor and declaring Emmy the winner by knockout in the first round. Then he turned to me and whispered, "Smart girl."

Ali made his first visit to Mantle's on a paid appearance for a large pharmaceutical company. During the schmooze-and-booze-a-thon, he seemed remote, dull, and listless. He was visibly shaking from the damage sustained during his heroic yet perilous boxing career. He would always be The Greatest, but it was sad to see him that way. An odd combination of pity and reverence hung thick in the air, and people clearly had mixed feelings about meeting him.

When the event was over, Ali's handler, famed photographer Howard Bingham, waved me over and told me that Ali wanted to go into the kitchen to meet the crew. This was the first time in the restaurant's history that any celebrity had asked to meet the back-of-house guys. (Since then, only Richard "The King" Petty has made such a request.)

Ali shuffled into the kitchen and greeted Chef Michael, as well as all the cooks and dishwashers individually. During this process, he spent extra time whispering words of solidarity into the ears of Muslim staff members. Then, just as the entire crew was getting misty-eyed, Ali asked them all if they wanted to see him "walk on air." Who wouldn't?

He stepped back from the crowd in order to create space and paused in front of the salad station, using that bit of floor as his makeshift stage. Being a nonbeliever in general, I dropped down on all fours to watch his feet. Ali wiggled his body and shook his hands, and then suddenly he was airborne. From my bird's-eye view, I could clearly see several inches of space between his feet and the white kitchen tiles.

The kitchen guys went berserk and broke into chants of, "A-li, A-li," their eyes wide with absolute awe. Ali returned to earth and threw his signature right-left combo as he danced backward out the swinging doors of the kitchen. The kitchen guys followed him out into the verboten dining area and then into the street, still chanting his name as a long, black limousine swallowed him up. Do you believe in magic? Yes!

Ousted OJ

Before his spectacular fall from grace, OJ Simpson was an American hero: superstar athlete, movie actor, and everybody's best pal. Even his Hertz Rent-a-Car commercial was a Madison Avenue legend. Back then, nobody knew about his dark side; rather, he was a Heisman Trophy winner, Hall-of-Fame running back, and burgeoning movie star. To me, his crowning cinematic achievement was his portrayal of Nordberg in *The Naked Gun*. (His free fall down the stadium steps in a wheelchair is hilarious time and time again, even more so now after OJ has been disgraced.)

In the mid-1990s, he owned a condo in the Trump Park Hotel on the corner of Sixth Avenue and Central Park South. He was in town three or four nights a week to appear on an NFL pre-game show and was a regular at Mickey's. It was on one of these occasions that I got to know the man who would one day respond to his wife's murder by taking a nationally televised fugitive-ride down the freeway in his white Ford Bronco, complete with body bag and shovel in the back.

Other than that, all I can say is that the first thing I noticed about OJ was his ridiculously large head. It was undoubtedly the largest I had ever seen, even bigger than San Francisco skipper Bruce Bochy—something like 50 percent bigger than a normal head, according to my calculations.

So one day, while sitting in Mickey's booth, facing the front door, OJ spied a beautiful young blond. At the time, OJ was riding high in Hollywood with his weekly HBO series, *First and Ten,* a groundbreaking success. Brimming with confidence, he laid down his mack: "Hey, baby," he murmured in a buttery baritone, "how would you like to guest star on my HBO series, *First and Ten?*"

Happy as could be, OJ's newest leading lady slid into the booth next to him, ready for stardom to befall her.

Just as the two of them were starting to get jiggy with it, who should appear at the entrance but Nicole Brown Simpson, scanning the room for her philandering husband like a quarterback picking up a blitzing safety. He saw her before she saw him, leapt over the back of the booth, and scrambled into the kitchen like he was running through airports. Then he juked through the basement and disappeared into the bowels of the building, surfacing like a gopher through the delivery hatch in the rear of the restaurant.

As soon as OJ had fled the coop, I sat down across from the bewildered bimbo in order to pinch-hit for him in his sudden absence.

Nicole stopped at our table and asked me if I had seen OJ.

"No," I lied. "Not today."

I felt badly for her as she stood there before me with a hollow, injured look in her eyes. Clearly, her bullshit meter was in full working order, and she glared at me for a couple of seconds before noticing the star-struck blond cowering sheepishly in the corner.

"Yeah, right," she said tersely. "He's been here." She then hustled indignantly out of Mickey's in search of her AWOL husband, finding about as much success as the Juice has had in his search for the true killer.

Toxic LT

There are at least two Lawrence Taylors. One is a polite Southern gentleman who chats with fans, signs autographs, and cheerfully poses for photos. This LT is a handsome and well-dressed Superman bursting with charisma. The other LT is a drunken, strung out, misogynistic womanizer with a terminal case of potty mouth. We'll call him "Toxic LT." He dropped by Mickey's one afternoon during his glory days with the Giants. As usual, a diamond-studded crucifix dangled from his left earlobe, but his formerly friendly face was now an angry mask of drunken rage.

Without waiting to be seated, he and a friend plunked themselves down at a table. LT was wearing leather pants, a slinky black T-shirt, and a black leather jacket to match. From the giddy-up, they were loud and obnoxious, cursing like longshoremen in a restaurant filled with women and children. The young model/actress assigned to his table approached to take his order. But Toxic LT wasn't hungry, and Toxic LT wasn't thirsty. Toxic LT was *horny*. As the lovely launched into the specials of the day, Toxic LT reached around, grabbed her ass with his gigantic paw, and growled, "That's what I'm talking about!" Appalled, the server left the table in tears, never to return.

A relief server was called in from the bullpen, and (surprise, surprise) LT immediately took a shine to her as well. Pulling her down into his lap, he asked her what the "real" specials were that day. She let out a yelp and leapt out of his grasp like an angry cat, kicking him in the shin and running for the kitchen. Now nobody wanted to wait on him, and after massaging his leg for a few minutes as though the kick to the shin had ended his season, Toxic LT summoned me over to his table, wanting to know why he couldn't "get any service in this place."

"Because this is a restaurant, not a whorehouse," I told him flatly. He was out of control, and if I was a referee, he would have been ejected.

Toxic LT gave me the hairy eyeball for a moment and then turned to his buddy. "Hey," he growled ominously, "I got an idea."

"LT," his friend replied warily, "when you get an idea, I get nervous."

I don't know what he had in mind, but thank God they both got up and left to seek adventure elsewhere. To be fair, it should be noted that Lawrence Taylor and not Toxic LT made several subsequent appearances at Mantle's and behaved like a perfect gentleman.

Wilt the Womanizer

Wilt "The Stilt" Chamberlain is simply the largest man I have ever encountered. Some guys like Jabbar, Finkel, and Manute Bol are taller. Some guys like The Fridge carry wider loads. But for a combo job of all-around grandeur, there is the rest of the world and then there was Wilt, may he rest in peace—a fiercely prideful man of seven feet four inches with thick, pronounced eyebrows and an aquiline nose. Yet somehow, his attributes worked in his favor, and he was generally regarded as devilishly handsome by men and women alike.

In 1992, Wilt came to Mickey's to host a signing for his new book, *Wilt,* in which he claimed to have made sweet love to upward of 10,000 women. I knew he was popular with the ladies, but ten grand wasn't a figure I was prepared to swallow, NBA legend or no.

On the night of the signing, the ladies' man strolled into Mickey's clad in a black-and-gold-striped shirt of shimmering silk and a pair of supple alligator shoes. Apart from his threads, Wilt kept it simple: nary a tattoo could be found on his person, and unlike many other NBA legends, he wore no bling. He simply sported a single, gold medallion, which hung from his tree-trunk neck by a hearty, spiral-carved chain. He wasn't trendy or overwrought, but stately and immaculate with a dollop of raw masculinity, something like James Bond meets Jimmy Brown.

He obliged my request for a photograph, and as the two of us posed together at seven-four and six feet respectively, customers stared and kitchen staff peeked out from behind the swinging kitchen doors. *Holy shit,* everyone seemed to be saying, *it's fucking Wilt Chamberlain, the only man ever to score a hundred points in an NBA game! The only man ever to have sexual relations with 10,000 women!*

After the photo-op, Wilt and I turned to each other and became locked in each other's gaze; it was like a *who-the-fuck-are-you* festival. I crumbled under the pressure of his steely glare and broke the silence.

"Wilt," I queried, resorting to humor as a defense mechanism, "the math just doesn't work out. *Ten thousand* women? I'm thinking ten thousand rolls in the hay divided by thirty years equals three hundred and thirty three women per year; that's like a new piece of ass for every day of the week!"

Wilt's stone-cold stare dissolved into a sly grin, his thick, well-manicured mustache spreading away from his mouth to reveal a sturdy set of neon-white teeth.

"Bill," he countered, "you don't understand. They used to line up outside my hotel room door."

"Well . . . why?" I asked him, after a brief pause.

Somewhat miffed by the question, he answered in an icy whisper, "Yo, man, when you're endowed like I am, the ladies tend to be very, *very* curious."

But wait . . . "Maybe so," I told him, "but just one follow-up question: who's gonna wanna be number ten thousand and one?"

16

TRICKS OF THE TRADE

Mickey was the master of practical jokes. He learned the trade early on in his tenure with the Yankees and plied it to perfection to his final days. In his last known stunt, he sent world-famous memorabilia collector Barry Halper an autographed bag of feces from his hospital room at Baylor University Hospital in Dallas, complete with brown-tipped latex examination gloves, as if to say that Barry would collect absolutely anything he could get his paws on. Barry turned the joke around on me the next day when he pulled up in front of the restaurant exalting, as per usual, that he had some "great shit" to show me in the trunk of his car. Normally, the trunk would open to reveal a game-worn Mantle jersey or perhaps the tar-stained bat from that controversial George Brett home run at Yankee Stadium. Imagine my absolute disgust when Barry opened his trunk to reveal his new treasure.

"Yuck, that smells like shit," I said.

"That's because it is shit—Mickey's shit."

In order to be a world-class practical joker, you must master the following skills, all of which are essential to the trade.

1. An impenetrable poker face: Novices will often succumb to the giggles at a critical stage in the game and blow their cover.

2. A predatory instinct: A world-class practical joker knows exactly which buttons to push, and when, on any given mark.

3. Charisma and leadership: An expert will sometimes need to enlist third and fourth parties in the canard, sometimes without their knowledge.

4. Ingenuity: Plans sometimes need to be changed on the fly when the unexpected occurs.

5. The patience of a saint: A practical joker must know how to let the joke play out until it's ripe enough to burst open on its own.

6. Maturity: Knowing how to draw the line when the fun stops.

For Mickey's part, when he wasn't punking me, he was punking other people with me as his wingman. I loved being in cahoots with my childhood hero. Among my most cherished memories of the Mick were times when he gave me "the look," not a wink, per se, but a special, fleeting glance to let me know that the games were about to begin.

In Mickey's absence, I practiced my new trade on my own, first looking for easy targets and working my way up to the more challenging marks. Somewhere along the line, I zeroed in on Jay Johnstone, baseball's unofficial merry prankster. Jay is so into the art of practical joking that he's even written a couple of books on the subject, including *Temporary Insanity* and *Over the Edge*. He was an above-average player for more than twenty seasons in the bigs, with teams such as the Yanks, Dodgers, Phillies, and White Sox. His lifetime stats are decent enough (102 home runs and a lifetime batting average of .276), but I believe it was his ability to crack people up and keep the team loose that kept him on the Major League rosters for so many years. To me, his greatest career moment occurred not in an actual game, but in the film *The Naked Gun*, when he strikes out looking on three pitches, with Leslie Nielsen behind the plate.

Once or twice a month, Jay would bounce into Mantle's looking for a freebie or the chance to pick up a quick appearance fee. I always made him feel right at home, but that didn't stop him from trying to play me. In the days before everyone and their great, great grandma had cellular phones, the restaurant had a portable phone for use at the tables. Jay came toward me one day with the now-obsolete appliance, announcing that I had a phone call. No sooner had I pressed it to my ear than Vaseline squirted out between my face and hand, leaving a trail of goop in its wake. Jay had smeared the handset beforehand. On a practical joke scale of 1 to 10, I thought this was worth maybe a 3, at best. Jay, however, thought it was an 11, and he quaked with laughter, gasping for air and stumbling around like he'd just been shot, before falling on the floor playing dead.

Payback time came when Jay was up for a coveted play-by-play position with the Phillies, one of his former teams. While he was in the men's room, I opened his stainless steel briefcase and stuffed a couple of raw burger patties into the side pocket, between a sheaf of papers and an abridged baseball almanac. Then I shut the case and left it right where I had found it, gleaming in the postmeridian sun that poured through the windows in the front dining room.

At this point, a novice prankster craving instant gratification would prod Jay to open his case and discover the meat (see rule 5). I let him leave without any mention of the briefcase or its secret cargo, and I had nearly forgotten about it by the time it detonated several days later.

Jay happened upon the aging, rotting beef during his interview with the Phillies. As he later explained it to me, the meeting had been outstanding until they'd asked him for a copy of his resumé—a formality, he presumed. Happy to oblige, Jay popped open his silver bullet and unleashed the olfactory fury of three-day-old hamburger patties in the advanced stages of decomposition. Of course, the suits at the interview had no idea what was causing the stench and could only imagine what sort of rotting carcass Johnstone was toting around in his briefcase. Sadly, he didn't get the job. I don't think I can fairly be blamed for the turn of events, but I suppose we'll never know.

Then there's my buddy Matt Weinberg, who owns a body shop called Heavenly Body Works in Maspeth, Queens. It's a thriving business, and Matt happens to be quite wealthy: the boat, the mansion in Great Neck, the country home in East Hampton, three late-model Mercedes, and a cache of diamond-encrusted Rolexes. Not bad for a garage guy. "I'm the poorest big-earner I know," he once said to me. I'm not sure what that means, but it can't be too shabby.

One day Matt called me at work to let me know that "Sherman," his lawyer, would be attending a Citibank-sponsored luncheon at Mantle's.

Matt's marching orders: "I want you to fuck with Sherman, big time."

I told Matt that I didn't even know the guy.

"Not to worry," Matt replied, "he'll be the fattest man in the room. There's no mistaking him."

"What should I do to him?" I inquired.

The restaurant's namesake, Mickey Mantle (left), with Patrick Ewing (middle) and author, at Mantle's after a Patrick Ewing press conference. (Liederman and Ewing are having bad hair days.)

With Wilt "The Stilt" Chamberlain after Wilt appeared on WFAN Radio to promote his last book boasting sexual conquests. 10,000 women, come on Wilt!

The author with Rod Gilbert, the other number 7, at the celebration of the Rangers' Stanley Cup victory in 1994.

With Otis Anderson at a party to celebrate his
Super Bowl MVP in 1991.

With the late
Boom Boom
Geoffrion after a
press conference
at Mickey
Mantle's.

With Don King shortly after a group of 100 Japanese tourists gave him a standing ovation in Mantle's. King responded, "Only in America."

With Sugar Ray Leonard as he prepares to appear on WFAN Radio after his victory over "No Mas" Roberto Durand.

With George Foreman after he regained the heavyweight title against Michael Moorer in 1994 at 45 years of age.

Muhammad Ali, after entering the kitchen at Mantle's to meet the staff. He is the only celebrity other than Richard "the King" Petty to make a similar request.

Flanked by Willis Reed and the late Dave DeBusshere at an event commemorating their last championship in 1973 at Mantle's.

The author poses between Manhattan Theatre Club's creative director Lynne Meadow and actor Adam Arkin at the opening-night party at Mickey Mantle's.

Mickey clowning with the author at Mickey's Fantasy Baseball Camp in Ft. Lauderdale, Florida.

Author, after having his "bell rung" at Mickey Mantle's Fantasy Baseball Camp in Ft. Lauderdale, Florida.

The author being interviewed by Pablo Guzman on CBS to explain changing the name of Mickey Mantle's to Ted Williams after the Red Sox came back from a 3-0 deficit to beat the Yankees in the American League Championship Series in 2004.

Two police cars are stationed for the weekend in front of Mantle's after the Ted Williams hoax.

"Whatever," he said. "Just make it good."

"Any boundaries?" I asked.

"No boundaries," he replied.

He didn't have to tell me twice.

Once the program had gotten under way, I scanned the banquet area. Weighing in at about half a metric ton, Sherman was easy to pick out of the crowd of one hundred-plus bankers, athletes, and accountants who were there to mingle, network, and stroke their existing clientele. He was seated at a table for eight, waiting to be served along with the other guests.

No boundaries, Matt's voice echoed.

I told the waiter to serve everyone except Sherman. Out came the salad, and then the appetizer, to all but one guest. By the time the main course came around, Sherman was twitching in his seat. Something along the lines of *FEED ME* was plainly churning, mantra-style, through his head as he stared eagerly at the kitchen door like a dog scratching on the screen, begging to get fed.

Just as Sherman was about to rip the waiter a new one, I had the kitchen send out no less than three raw, thick-cut T-bone steaks piled high on a silver tray.

"WEINBERG," Sherman seethed as the meat was set before him. "I'm going to kill that motherfucker!"

When he excused himself from the table, all the other guests had to step away from their seats and away from the table to let him out free at last. He then asked to speak to a manager.

"That would be me," I fibbed, so as to spare the real manager a scathing inquisition. "I'm sorry, Mr. Sherman. Matt Weinberg put me up to it."

"That's what I thought," Sherman grunted, whipping a cell phone from beneath his roll of lard and speed-dialing his antagonist.

"You cocksucker!" he shouted into the phone. "You humiliated me in front of my clients. And speaking of clients, you are no longer a client of mine, so find yourself a new fucking lawyer, you fucking asshole."

Without another word, he flipped his phone shut and hurtled out the front door.

Weinberg called me back right away.

"You fucked me," he cried, "you went too far!"

"You told me there were no boundaries, remember?"

"Yeah," he seethed, "but you went *beyond* no boundaries. Even no boundaries have boundaries."

"I *need* Sherman," Matt persisted. "I'm involved in a massive lawsuit with Mr. Glass. Now what the fuck am I gonna do?"

"Get a new lawyer . . . ," I suggested lamely.

"What, and shell out a ton of money to bring him up to speed? Great, why didn't I think of that myself?"

"I don't know what to tell you," I faltered, scratching my head. I was starting to feel like a real shit heel.

"What would you do if you were me?" Matt wanted to know.

"If I were you . . . ," I stalled, mulling it over, "I would send him a gift at the office, along with a note of apology."

"What sort of a gift?"

"Something dignified," I said. "Why don't you send him one of those Montblanc pens you keep in your desk drawer?"

"You mean the fake ones . . . ? That's not bad," he mused, and hung up without another word.

The next day, Matt had the fake pen along with a dozen roses delivered to Sherman with a handwritten note groveling for forgiveness. Sherman accepted the apology and took Matt back as a client.

No discussion about practical joking is complete without allusion to King, a crewcutted ex-Marine from Clearwater, Florida, who served a decade at Mantle's as the director of operations. King is a good guy, a good manager, and an upright citizen with a great heart. After I interviewed him for the position, I called a manager I knew from the same restaurant as King to see what she thought of her one-time colleague. "He's . . . a real dedicated guy," she managed. "His biggest problem is that he cares too much and gets far too emotionally involved."

I like someone with passion for his work, so despite his colleague's spotty recommendation, I considered him a viable candidate. I narrowed the search down to him and one other applicant. She actually wet her pants during the interview, and King got the job.

Life with King was like an emotional tilt-a-whirl. He'd get mad, he'd lash out, he'd get remorseful, and he'd apologize profusely. As a ramrod of an ex-Marine, he was both good and bad for business: good because he kept the place squared away like a military barracks, and bad because his unchecked temper was a real liability.

One snowy day in December 2003, in walked Bethany Hamilton, the surfer girl who had recently lost her arm to a shark with the munchies on Hawaii's famed North Shore. King spotted her right away from his outpost at the front desk and pointed her out to me.

"King," I said, "she should be done with her lunch in about an hour. That means you have roughly fifty-five minutes to come up with a surfboard that she can sign for the restaurant. Ready, set, go."

Sure enough, a snow-covered King returned to Mickey Mantle's forty-five minutes later with a glossy new short-board in tow. Bethany's father agreed to let her sign it, providing the board would remain on display at the restaurant and never be sold.

"To Mickey Mantle's," she scrawled with her remaining hand, "my favorite sports restaurant! Love, Bethany Hamilton." Then she posed next to the board for a photograph, which I had framed and mounted and placed alongside the board for display the very next day.

In the weeks that followed, King reminded me ten times too many about the oath to never sell the board. "Okay, King, point well taken," I said, "and besides, who'd want to buy a surfboard made out to Mickey Mantle's?"

"I suppose you're right," he admitted, "but just in case, I wanted to remind you."

The following Monday, I had an Australian acquaintance of mine call the restaurant and ask for the general manager. When King came to the phone, the guy introduced himself as the lawyer for Greg "The Shark" Norman, the pro golfer, and explained that because of his nickname, Norman wanted the shark victim's board for his personal collection of quirky and unusual keepsakes.

"It's not for sale," King answered a little too loudly, as per usual.

"Not even to one of the world's wealthiest sportsmen?" my friend from Down Under wanted to know.

"Not even for a million bucks," King insisted rhetorically.

"How about a million-one?"

"*No*," King snapped, and hung up the phone.

A couple days hence, I confided in King about the increasingly dire condition of our finances in the wake of the 9/11 disaster. "Sell whatever memorabilia you can," I reminded him. "We need the money, *bad*."

"Right . . . ," he replied slowly, "any memorabilia except for the surfboard, of course."

"Please," I fretted, "we should *be* so lucky as for someone to want to buy that stupid-ass thing."

I could sense, as I meandered away, that King was experiencing some emotional pain. He'd refused an offer that could potentially save him his job and the restaurant, and he'd been rude about it to boot. On the other hand, he'd given his word to the one-armed child and her dad, and he didn't see fit to go back on it.

"Well," he began, nipping at my heels, "there is just one guy . . . one Greg 'The Shark' Norman, if you will . . ."

"King, what are you saying to me?" I asked him, massaging my temples and sinking down into my chair as though under the weight of some great burden. "Did someone make a bid on the surf-board?"

"Shark Norman," he blurted, unable to contain it a moment longer. "I mean—er—Mr. Gregory Norman expressed a passing interest in purchasing the board."

"A passing interest," I said. "What's a passing interest?"

"He made me an offer."

"How much?"

"Over a million dollars," King admitted.

"*A million dollars?*" I squealed, leaping from my seat and dancing a little jig of disbelief. "A million dollars would solve all of our problems. Call him right now and do the deal!"

"Bill," he replied, "I have always admired your honesty and integrity. How can you sell that surfboard when we promised that poor girl . . . ?"

"King, for a million bucks we could give half to her favorite charity, kick six figures back to her, and *still* have enough left over to pay our bills. MAKE THE CALL!"

"But Bill," he wailed, "please don't do this to me. I just *can't* sell the board. I gave Bethany my word of honor! Please, as a favor to me, at least take a few days to think it over."

I rubbed my brow a bit before agreeing to mull it over.

Two days later, I asked King to give me the number for Greg Norman's lawyer and let me work it out.

"Bill . . . ," he floundered, "I don't have the number. I . . . I thought it was a moot point."

"A million-dollar *moot point?* Where did you toss it?"

"I . . . I never took it down."

"Well, *get it*, for the love of Bob! I don't care what it takes; just get me the million-dollar phone number!"

I ran up to my apartment, called the Australian guy back, and got him to call King again, later that day, saying he'd just spoken to me and that I had agreed to sell him the board for a cool million and when should he come by to pick it up?

"No way," King roared, "that surfboard leaves this restaurant over my dead body!" It sounded like the Marine credo of no man left behind.

As I listened in on the line, I pictured King as Charlton Heston for the NRA, holding a surfboard high above his head before a sea of applauding zealots and shouting, *From my cold, dead hands!* Apparently, King was determined never to sell the board, no matter what I said or did.

Early the next morning, I went downstairs and enlisted one of the doormen to write the following note to King:

> *Dear King,*
>
> *I stopped by early as per Bill's instructions and picked up the surfboard. I'm flying it back to Melbourne today, and will forward the check as soon as I get there. If you need to reach me, call Shark Enterprises in Sidney, Australia. Thanks again.*

Then I took the board down off the wall and pinned up the note in its place. I hid the board in my apartment and waited for King to arrive at the scene of the crime. I watched him take note of the surfboard's glaring absence, tear the note from the barren patch of wall, and storm back through the kitchen down to the office. The banquet manager was already down there that morning, and I called him on the intercom about half a minute later.

"Let me guess what King is doing right now," I offered.

"What's that?"

"I'll bet you a million bucks that *right now*, King is calling the operator to get the country code for Australia. Am I right?"

"That's amazing," he marveled, "how did you know that?"

I let Banquet Man in on the joke. Driven by his sense of born-again protocol, he immediately sang to King, pulling the plug on my hoax.

A few minutes later, King rocketed out of the restaurant and into the park to clear his head. Everyone had a good laugh at his expense, which is never taken lightly by someone with anger-management issues.

But life goes on. The next day, he told me he'd known all along I would never sell the board, because, as he put it, my word was "stronger than oak."

17

SHORT STAY RATE

ONCE UPON A TIME there was a small kiddie play area in the back room of Mantle's—just a few toys and books to keep the young'ns occupied before the meal, a time that I (a dad four times over) call the purest form of torture. It's that magical interlude between the time when you place the order and the food arrives, during which the kids spill their drinks, spill *your* drinks, toss the silverware around, poke one another, and whine about being hungry and bored.

One of the toys in the kiddie area was a three-by-three-foot plastic house with a red roof, blue shutters, and a red arch-shaped front door. Sounds pretty simple, but the kids go ape-shit for it.

You may or may not remember how in the summer of 2002, a buxom, bleached-blond Yankees fan hopped over the fence at Yankee Stadium and gave Derek Jeter her phone number on a scrap of paper. She caused a big stir with the media and got her fifteen minutes. She was pictured on the front page of the *Post* and the *Daily News*, and on all the evening news programs, slipping Jeter her digits. That season, she was a fixture on the B-list sports party circuit.

There was a fund-raising event at Mickey's a couple weeks after the incident, and she was on the freebie list. She arrived solo, decked out in a glittery cocktail frock. Grinning and tossing her hair, she schmoozed like a pro, mingling, meandering, and scoping her avenues and flirting with man after man as if she had a sign on her head that read, "Fuck me, now."

Later, as the clock struck midnight, the event ended, and Mantle's started to empty out. King (of the surfboard snafu) was managing that evening, and as he went to kill the lights, close up, and go home to his wife and infant daughter, he heard panting from the plastic playhouse. The red door and the blue plastic shutters were closed, and the house quaked from within.

As he drew closer, the sounds of wanton lovemaking began to rise from the tiny love shack: *Oh baby, fuck me, fuck me harder*, and the like.

King reached a fork in the road as he knew the customer is always right, and he wanted to be hospitable, but at the same time, he was all about good family values and propriety, and he couldn't allow people to hit skins where toddlers play house. Unsure of how to proceed, King knocked gingerly on the miniature plastic door.

"Excuse me . . . the party has ended, and I have to close up."

"Hey, pal, take a hike," a man's voice gasped from within. "I'm not done yet."

King obliged them and made himself scarce for a couple of minutes, but to no avail. The fuck-fest raged on interminably.

"Hey, there," King shouted, slapping the plastic rooftop for emphasis, "it's time to throw in the towel, there, sir. Alrighty? It's time to call it a night."

The bedraggled twosome emerged from the no-tell motel like beetles from beneath an overturned rock. King quaked with anticipation as they reluctantly unfurled themselves to reveal their true forms. The man turned out to be a six-foot-six professional football player from one of the NIT teams. The woman turned out to be none other than the Derek Jeter fanatic, with her sequined minidress up over her ears, Paris Hilton–style. The two of them hit the bricks, leaving a used condom on the floor of the kiddie love shack. Now that's class. Derek, lose that number!

18

SHITTING WHERE YOU EAT

ANY WORKPLACE ENVIRONMENT can become a breeding ground for romance, sex, love, and even marriage, but working in a restaurant more than quadruples the odds. In a typical office environment, colleagues daydream, from the privacy of their own cubicles, and meet at the water cooler. In a restaurant, employees are on the move, mingling freely with whomever it is they fancy. In a place like Mantle's, the servers are mostly aspiring actors and models, which makes for an unusually attractive staff. Now you've got a bunch of charismatic, twenty-something lookers strutting around the restaurant, piquing each other's interest. Yowza.

Of course, an all-hottie staff is great for attracting new customers and keeping old ones. Perky waitresses come to work in their best push-up bras and shortest skirts in the hope that Steven Spielberg would sit in their section. *Hello, there, Brandy. How would you like to star in my next major motion picture?* Hey, it could happen. I heard Cameron Diaz got discovered that way.

Acting-impaired servers hope to impress wealthy executives who'll pop rings onto their manicured fingers and whisk them off to mansions in East Egg, which brings me to the first of three main categories of restaurant romance: server to customer.

When a waitress is smitten, she'll linger at the table just a little longer than necessary. "What *else* can I get you?" she'll say, in a tone reminiscent of Marilyn Monroe at the *Some Like It Hot* pajama party. It's comical to watch the guys cover up their wedding bands with their meat hands and then drop the rings into their shirt pockets when nobody's looking, exposing a tan line.

Sometimes a waitress will leave a little note inside the check presenter: *Nice meeting you. Hope to see u soon. XXOX Jenny (212-687-5309)*

Some schmucks will reciprocate by leaving their business cards on the table. Some slip the young lady their card on the way out. Cowardly Casanovas leave their cards with the manager for special delivery.

The problem with this sort of relationship is that it almost always results in the loss of a good customer. When the relationships sour, the customers would rather chow down at the trough with a barnyard of hogs than visit the restaurant. Or worse yet, they'll haunt the place, stalking their prey until we have to throw them out for good. I've seen many Romeos attempt to access her schedule by pumping hostesses for information.

"Is Tiffany working tonight?" they'll ask.

"No, not tonight."

"Well, when is she working next?"

Ever helpful, the hostess usually coughs up the info. One lothario walked away with a copy of the schedule and all the staff phone numbers, courtesy of our eager-to-please hostess.

If cloak-and-dagger techniques don't work, the pushy suitor will wait at the bar until the hostess steps away from the desk and steal the phone list right out of the coat closet. Next thing you know, the entire staff is getting dirty phone calls from some freak-show sports-bar groupie. Servers storm into work, pounding the bar with their fists, crying hysterically and demanding to know who gave Ted Bundy their phone numbers.

I've seen guys stand across the street with high-powered binoculars, phony mustaches—the whole nine. In extreme scenarios, we've helped servers get restraining orders to protect them from the Big Bad Wolf.

In the early days, this one weirdo was stalking a bartender named Joan. He started out as an occasional customer but soon became a regular, taking all of his meals at the bar with Joan during her shifts. Always a sweetheart, she put up with him, until one day she returned home to find him sitting on her front stoop. She got a restraining order against him. He began spooking the place on her days off. He purchased one of every piece of logo apparel we had in the shop and arrived dressed head to toe in Mantle's gear.

Before long, Mickey got wind of what had happened with Joan. The next time her stalker came to the bar, Mickey dragged him out back into the courtyard, out of the way of prying eyes. "Listen, asshole," he said, slamming the man up against the garden wall. "The next time you set foot in my restaurant, I'll give you a whuppin' you'll never for-git."

The stalker started sobbing and slobbering.

"Get a hold of yourself and get the fuck out of here, asshole."

Old Western justice at its finest.

The next category of restaurant romance is server to server. At last count, more than twenty marriages have resulted from Mantle's intramural meat market. This is astounding, given the female-heavy gender ratio. If a waiter is straight, friendly, and the least bit attractive, he's a bull running through a herd of cows in mating season. Belt notches accumulate at warp speed. Some go to great lengths to keep their conquests a national secret. Some, like the legendary Mick Royal, just don't give a flying fuck. Mick would juggle three or four waitresses at a time.

Before Mick, there was Ryan, a clean-cut, white-toothed, Jason Priestley type of a guy. More often than not, he'd come into work with a smug little grin that I came to know as the freshly laid look.

"Okay," I asked him one morning, "who was last night?"

"Oh, Bill," he replied, "you know I can't tell you that. But I will: it was Lauren!"

"But Ryan," I said, "that's not news. You've been doing her for weeks."

"Yeah," he said, "but this was the first time I did her in the locker room, during a shift. Don't worry—I got someone to watch my tables."

"That was good of you."

"Wait, there's more," he said.

"There's *more?*"

Ryan went on to explain that in fact there was a third party on top of the laundry pile in the locker room.

I launched into the mandatory follow-up questions: who did what to whom, and so forth.

"Everyone did everything to everybody," he gushed. "It was so, like, totally all good."

"Well, in the future," I suggested, "let's keep it out of the locker room."

"Sure," he agreed, "how about the boiler room or the walk-in box?"

A few weeks later, I ran into a regular at a charity event.

"Hey, man," he said, "I bought a menu at your place last night. The price was seven dollars, but I got a much better deal from my waiter: only four dollars in cash, right at the table. Nice guy, that Ryan."

Stop thief! I trumped early the next day.

Lauren put herself through law school while at Mantle's and then opened a restaurant with Ryan.

This is another kind of love connection that takes place on Central Park South—the kind that is paid for in cash.

A man-child named Chris has been working at Mickey's as a porter since 1989. He's not retarded, per se, and he doesn't have Down syndrome or any obvious congenital defects. He's kind of a Forrest Gump type, but for all I know, he could have a high IQ. He's skittishly nervous and has the naiveté of an eleven-year-old boy in a forty-something body, thrown into the workforce to sink or swim.

He compensates with an eager spirit and a randomly cultivated vocabulary: *Yes, indeed, Mr. Liederman . . . Everything looks copacetic, Mr. Liederman. Yes indeed, yes indeed.* Moreover, he's a sweet guy, and despite his idiosyncrasies, Chris is the most loyal and dedicated employee that has ever worked for me in my thirty years of hiring restaurant people. When shipments arrived, he'd count out the entire order piece by piece. When a box supposedly containing one hundred lemons would came down the delivery hatch, he'd count each and every one of them while the driver waited for his signature, with the truck running.

With Chris keeping score, drivers had to cease their time-honored tradition of shorting the orders and selling the pilfered goods at a deep discount to the next stop on their route. Deliveries took twice as long with Chris on the receiving end. White Plains Linen actually offered a 10 percent discount if Chris would stop counting napkins. We accepted the offer, but like the Count on Sesame Street, he kept counting. Once, I had to pull the driver from White Plains Linen off of Chris as he attempted to strangle him.

The brazen I-don't-give-a-fuck delivery guys heaped on the abuse. "Hey, Rain Man," they'd taunt, "count that shit and let me get the fuck out of here, retard."

Despite their cruel remarks, the drivers never weakened Chris's resolve. He'd get rattled, but only a little bit, as he puttered on, counting the goods. *N-ninety eight, n-ninety nine, one-one hundred—oh! Indeed! One hundred lemons. Alrighty. Thank you, sir.* He always called everyone sir.

After he had worked for me for about three years, Chris slinked into the office one day with Ross, our manager, who stood beside him with a bemused expression.

"Bill," Ross explained, "Chris has something he would like to ask you."

"Okay," I said, "lay it on me."

Chris could barely meet my eyes as he hopped back and forth from one foot to the other and wrung his hands, trying to find his voice, looking as if he was having a bathroom emergency.

"It's okay, Chris," Ross coaxed, "Bill's listening. Go ahead."

"Well, Mr. Liederman, sir," Chris began, "I was wondering if . . . I was w-wondering if, if . . . ohhhhh . . . I'd like to ask you for a r-raise, sir."

Ross let out a giggle, which he tried to disguise as a hacking cough. Clearly, he and Chris had rehearsed this exchange several times before they approached me.

"A raise," I said. "Well, that sounds fair. You've done a great job for us for the last three years. What kind of raise are you looking for?"

Chris exhaled and wiped his hands on his apron.

"I don't know," he gulped, "a nickel?"

Ross could no longer hide his amusement and neither could I. It was just about the dearest, sweetest, most innocent thing I had ever heard.

"A nickel an hour, eh? I'll tell you what, Chris, let's make it a dime."

"A *dime*," he squealed. "Alrighty then, Mr. Liederman, sir. Thank you, sir. Yes indeed!"

He balled his hands into fists and pummeled the air in triumph before scurrying out of the office.

The next day I had the bookkeeper add a dollar fifty an hour to Chris's salary.

Chris's colleagues at Mantle's always dug him, especially the dishwashers and cooks, as he was eager to do their work in addition to his regular duties for a couple of extra bucks a week. Even so, they couldn't help but tease him.

"Hey, Chris," they'd hoot, "are you a virgin? Have you ever kissed a girl? Sucked her titties? Fuck her in the coulo, maybe?"

"N-not yet, fellas," he'd giggle, blushing and ducking his head sideways and cockeyed.

One year, during the Christmas season, the "fellas" chipped in and got Chris a prostitute who owned the corner of Sixth Avenue and 58th Street. They escorted her down the delivery entrance and coaxed Chris into the Ménage-à-Trois Memorial Lady's Locker Room with her. Then they shut the door and pressed their ears up against it, straining to listen.

About a minute into it, the door burst open and the hooker scampered by the delivery entrance back out into broad daylight.

"Th-thanks, f-fellas," Chris gulped, standing up a little taller than before. "I really n-needed that."

19

BEGGAR'S BANQUET

THEY SAY NECESSITY is the mother of invention, and in the restaurant business, this is particularly true. For the restaurant owner, each day is a living lesson in Murphy's Law. Whatever can go wrong absolutely will go wrong, time and again. Broken dishwasher, burned-out kitchen exhaust fans, blown compressor in the walk-in boxes, inoperable beer taps, random computer failure, AWOL waiter, rogue food delivery, and dumbwaiter inspections from the City Department of the Dumb.

In most cases, you can circumvent disaster, either by paging the repair guy or enlisting the help of the building superintendent and letting him do what he does best: fix things with partially masticated gum and Band-Aids. When the repair guy doesn't answer your page and the Bazooka doesn't work, you have to take a deep breath and brace yourself for a day of coddling angry customers who are affected by this problem.

Here is a short list of things that can and will go wrong, and the corresponding do-it-yourself, in-house remedies.

Broken dishwasher: Wash dishes by hand.

Broken walk-in box: Order a ton of ice from the "rip-off" ice delivery service (that probably sent someone in, in the first place, to break the ice machine).

Broken phone: Use cell phone and pretend you're not losing dozens of reservations because callers believe the restaurant has closed.

Broken plate-glass window: Seat customers in the back, away from the door.

Ventilation system malfunction: Have waiters promote only salads—or anything else that doesn't get baked, fried, sautéed, roasted, or grilled.

Broken pipes in the basement: Fashion rafts out of delivery skids and use a mop handle Tom Sawyer–style to propel yourself between the walk-in box, the prep kitchen, and the delivery hatch.

Ceiling leaks: Get a bucket, rope off the problem area, and seat customers as far away from the leaks as possible.

Busted bar taps: Serve bottled beer and try to forget how much bigger the profit margin for draught beer is.

Broken dumbwaiter: Have all the prepped food hauled up the steps and hope that your porter doesn't become your partner by falling down the stairs under an avalanche of mashed potatoes.

Computer/register malfunction: Have a blast from the past with handwritten dupes and carbon-copied checks. Prepare to get pounded by your bearded lady of a bookkeeper when she arrives the next morning to encounter the financial mess you've created and to get howled at by a customer who, after an hour of waiting, gets a slice of cheesecake instead of a Philadelphia cheese steak.

Plumbing malfunction in guest bathroom: Bomb the place with air freshener and throw bags of road salt around the bathroom floor to stem the tide. Close the door and hang a little sign that reads: bathrooms under renovation. feel free to use the facilities next door at either the ritz-carlton or the park lane hotel. sorry for the inconvenience. Broken-down delivery truck: Haul ass to the supermarket and pay bust-out retail for the groceries you need.

The one problem you can't always buy or bargain away is an AWOL employee. You can start by attacking the phone list and trying to wrangle a substitute, or two or three, sometimes out of the same bed. One absent server, busser, or cook won't kill you. But two waiters short on a busy Saturday night means it's time to bust out the old apron and take the waiter in you for a spin. The waiter in *me* put me through college, so "would you like fries with that" is a phrase with which I'm well acquainted. Those who have never waited tables should not open restaurants.

If you're short a cook during holiday season, become the short-order cook: grab a spatula and start flipping burgers.

In the dreaded event that you're short a dishwasher, kitchen detail, *and* waitstaff on the same day, it is almost time for "game over" to flash on the TV screens. Short of covering the dirty spots on the plates with new food (a desperation move I learned on my first restaurant job), there's not a whole lot you can do—other than start screaming.

Enter One-Tooth Tony. Tony was a middle-aged panhandler who had first dibbs on the turf between the Plaza and the Ritz. His favorite post was directly in front of Mantle's.

His costume was like something out of *Oliver Twist*: pants slit vertically with scissors to denote a "tattered" quality, plastic bags for shoes, a length of yellow police tape for his belt, and, often as not, a pair of ratty men's briefs accessorizing his head. In summer, he wore no shirt, but in winter, he sported a plastic grocery bag with holes to accommodate his head and arms. The whole ensemble was desperately post-apocalyptic. The dude looked like an extra from the set of *Waterworld*. And to top it all off, One-Tooth Tony only had one tooth in his head.

Tony had a set of sales pitches that worked on the blue-haired lady tourists named Betty and their husbands named Bob: *Would you like to contribute to the Untied Negro College Fund?* was an old favorite; *Give me a hundred bucks so I can buy a good cup of coffee*, was another; or, *My wife and ten children are waiting for me to come home with something to eat; don't let my kids cry themselves to sleep.* (Of course, that was all a crock. Tony was a bachelor, but it didn't really matter whether you believed him or not. It was worth a buck just to get him to shut up and to stop following you up the block.) And a few more: *I'm an ex-Mantle's employee who can't collect his paycheck. Please spare some change so I can retain a lawyer and get what's due me; or, Help me get back on my feet so that I can go back to work as a computer technician.*

Sometimes he even wore primitive sandwich boards, just to mix it up. Hand-painted signs bearing slogans such as 5 DAYS TO LIVE, NEED LAST MEAL, or VIETNAM VET, WOUNDED IN DIEN BIEN PHU AND HAMBURGER HILL adorned his torso as he promenaded up and down the block, with both palms outstretched.

Oftentimes we tried to shoo him away when he harassed the customers, or the cops from Midtown North would whisk him away to a shelter. He had a stranglehold on the block, and the other neighborhood panhandlers knew not to tread on his turf. Sometimes new guys would try to take his spot in front of Mantle's, but only because they didn't know any better. Tony would hobble over to shoo them off—and they never came back. I've often imagined that at least some of these poor wretches now occupy a watery grave, having been dumped in the duck pond across the street for poaching on another man's begging turf.

We were minus a dishwasher on Black Friday, the day after Thanksgiving, otherwise known as the busiest restaurant and shopping day of the year. Just when I was starting to panic about finding a dishwasher, I happened to glimpse Tony through the plate glass windows, wearing his Vietnam sandwich boards and accosting my customers on their way out. It seemed almost perfect: I would have a dishwasher *and* a Tony-free storefront.

"Hey, Tony," I said, spinning madly through the revolving door, "how's business?"

"Kinda slow," he pouted, "how about spotting me a twenty?"

"How about washing some dishes for me? . . . I'm serious, Tony. Wash some dishes for me. It won't make you rich, but it's gotta be better than what you're making out here. You say you can't find a job—well here's a fucking job, for God's sake! C'mon, Tony, give it a go. What do you have to lose?"

"Cash only," he mumbled. "I don't take checks."

"Fine, cash, whatever. Just throw on some rubber gloves and let's get ready to rumble."

"I gotta get paid up front. It's my policy."

I reached into my pocket and pulled out a twenty.

"Here's an advance," I said. "Now go downstairs, put on a clean uniform, and start washing dishes. If you're still here at the end of the shift, I'll pay you the difference."

What can I say? I needed a damn dishwasher.

"How many hours am I guaranteed?"

Thinking that he'd probably limp away screaming after about forty-five minutes in the fast-paced dish room, I brushed the question off like a dockside dragonfly.

"As many as you want, Tony. You can work as long as you like."

And so it was that Tony came in off the streets and an understudy beggar magically appeared in his place.

Several times during our chock-a-block lunch hour, I shot past Tony to make sure he was still swishing and dishing the dishes. Working for money wasn't something he was accustomed to, so I didn't know what to expect.

Within his first hour of service, he had implemented a new system of garbage disposal. As the dirty plates were dumped in the dish area, he would shovel all the leftover food into his face. I quickly calculated that Tony's recycling method would save us at least a dollar a day on garbage bags and hauling fees. This guy was paying off like a one-armed bandit.

At the end of the shift, when all the dishes were washed and his work area was nice and tidy, I paid Tony and invited him to come back to work the next day. The social worker in me positively beamed. I had taken a broken man off the street and helped him back into the workforce.

"I got one problem and one question," Tony grunted, peeling off his long, yellow gloves.

"What's the problem?" I asked

"Ten dollars an hour is not enough. I average two hundred dollars a day out front on the street, and I ain't gotta wash no dishes out there."

"That *can't* be true," I argued, wondering to myself if, in fact, it could.

"What's the question?"

"Do I get dental insurance?"

"Tony," I replied, totally flabbergasted, "you only have one tooth."

"I'm outta here," he snapped, wriggling out of his apron and stomping off to fetch his sandwich boards and reclaim his stomping grounds.

20

GOOD RUBBISH

EARLY ON IN MY CAREER as a restaurant proprietor and operator of a restaurant school, people warned me that I'd be dealing with the Mafia on a day-to-day basis. It was understood around town that the local crew of goombas strong-armed every restaurant in the area, like in *Goodfellas: No business? Fuck you, pay me. Bad weather? Fuck you, pay me. Street construction blocking access to the front door? Fuck you, pay me.*

It was discouraging, but it turned out the rumors were wildly exaggerated. In reality, cartels only controlled two services used by the restaurant business: linens and garbage. Early on in construction, some representatives from the ABC hauling company paid me a visit at the site. There was Tony, his cousin Tone, and his father Antonio, all wearing shiny new suits.

Tony introduced himself by saying, "We *are* your garbage company. We service the entire block, exclusively."

"Right, okay," I said, rolling with the punches. "How much is this dirty work gonna cost me?"

"Sixty-five hundred a month," announced Tony Jr. (This was in 1987, before the city had busted up the garbage cartels, lowering our garbage price to $1,200 a month! It was the first time in restaurant history that prices actually went down.)

"Sixty-five hundred? That's almost a third of my entire rent."

The Tonys greeted this comment with steely glares.

"Take it, or leave all your stinking trash on the street," Tony snapped, and then the deal was done.

Then there were linens, the second no-fly zone. One day, Bruce of White Plains Linen showed up with a price list and announced that he would be servicing our linen account. At that time, we used tablecloths, as was the trend in upscale restaurants. Linen prices were astronomical: napkins, 9¢; tablecloths, 54¢; aprons, 25¢. As I ballpark calculated the cost of linens for a year, over the fifteen years of our lease, I figured I could save enough money to pay for one year at Princeton for my son, Mack. In a state of heightened sticker shock, I told him I'd get back to him and hoped he'd go away—but he wouldn't go away.

"Your only other option is not to use any linens at all, unless you plan to install your own laundry and clean your own shit."

"You can do that?"

"If you're crazy enough. I even know a guy who can hook it up for you, if that's what you want. I don't give a fuck."

The next day, a new group of guys named Tony arrived with a presentation on in-house linen laundering. I was hell-bent on making it work for Mickey Mantle's. I had been forced to turn over my garbage business to a bunch of goons, and I wasn't going to let it happen twice.

We set up the laundry operation right outside the men's locker room in the basement. It was a churning urn of burning funk, complete with washer, dryer, steam press, and a staff of three that came "recommended" by the linen company.

The results were disastrous. Linens came out spotted and warped into funny shapes and sizes. One day, in the middle of lunch service, smoke began to billow out of the laundry area. Flames engulfed the south end of the prep kitchen, setting off the ancillary system and spattering the entire prep area with white Ghostbuster goo. The fire department arrived just in time to save us and the rest of the twenty-story building from incineration. New York's Bravest did prevail, but not before our restaurant superintendent was rushed to the ER to be treated for smoke inhalation.

So much for doing our own laundry. White Plains Linen began service the next week. You don't piss on Superman's cape, and you don't mess with the linen guys . . . or they'll hang you and your napkins out to dry.

It wasn't until 2003 that the feds busted up the linen cartel for price fixing. The racket was simple: at weekly poker games, the wash 'n' dry boys would sit around like The Dirty Dozen, sucking on salami-sized stogies, sipping cognac, and setting prices. Over hand after hand of poker, they would hammer out who got what account. Once decreed, the linen routes were set in stone. The only way for a restaurant to switch linen companies was to find a replacement account of equal value for the linen company. A mere impossibility.

An interesting side note about linen prices: since 1988, they have neither risen nor fallen. Rather, they have stayed exactly the same and nobody seems to know why, except the wise guys.

In the early 1990s, business at Mickey's declined sharply because of the Gulf War. It was time to make an end run at some of our expenses, and my attention went straight to our lollapalooza garbage bill. I strapped on a pair of XXL balls and called the Tonys for a sit-down. My general manager reminded me that, "You can't negotiate with the garbage guys," but we simply couldn't afford the $6,500 monthly garbage bill.

My daughter Chloe was twelve years old at the time and already beginning to show signs of her dad's irreverent wit. She stopped by Mickey's after school that day, and as I seated myself at a booth with the Tonys, she joined the meeting as an uninvited guest. I tried to wave her off, but the Tonys wouldn't hear of it.

"She's such a cutie," they cooed. "Let her join da meeting. Aw, would you look at dat face? What a doll. She should be a movie star!"

"Yeah, sure, alright," I said, moving right along. "Look, guys, the fact is that we just can't survive paying your garbage bills, and we need to look at some other options." I went on to explain that we wanted a reduction in our monthly bill, which was better than nothing. Tony didn't flinch, knowing the next occupant would pay his price.

"We're not going to be able to pay you anything when we're closed," I reasoned.

"Your only uddah option is to leave your garbage in da middle of da street, stinking to high heaven, and wait for da tickets to start piling up," said Tony Jr.

Cousin Tone nodded solemnly. Anthony Sr. gnashed his teeth and grunted. Suddenly, Chloe came to realize what was going down.

"Wait a minute," she mused, her eyes twinkling with glee, "are you guys in the Mafia?"

There was no joy in Tonyville. For a moment, I thought about diving under the table. But now that my kid had said the M word, I decided to stand up and fight.

"Come on," I cajoled them, "gimme a break. How about I get each of you a Mickey Mantle autographed baseball, and you take half your fee each month in free food and booze. You and all your friends and family can eat here whenever you like. You'd be our honored guests."

My proposal was met with silence before Tony Jr. finally spoke. "Bill," he asked, "can you excuse us for a moment to discuss your proposal?"

"Take your time, take your time, take your time," I chanted.

They excused themselves from the table and huddled up near the bar, shooting us not-so-nice glances throughout their powwow. After several minutes, I could only assume they were discussing where they would dispose of my body parts.

"Guess maybe I shouldn't have said that Mafia thing," Chloe offered.

"Guess not, but don't worry about it. I'll fix it."

I hoped I sounded more confident than I felt.

A minute later, the Tonys returned and took turns slapping my back.

"You got yourself a fucking deal," Tony Jr. announced. "Long as you can get da balls made out to us *personal* by da Mick. You know, wit our names and shit . . ."

"Sure," I promised—my wait to exhale finally over.

The Tonys thanked me and left happy. The next day, Mickey came for lunch, and I plunked three brand-new regulation American League baseballs down in front of him.

"Who the fuck are these for?" he demanded.

"They're all for Tony," I said, giving him the short form.

"Bill," Mickey protested, "how many fucking times have ah told you, only one ball per customer."

I laughed and told him the entire story from beginning to end.

"Well," he surmised, "ah guess you really *can* negotiate with them boys."

"Yeah," I agreed. "They're pretty good fellas."

21

JOE PEPITONE'S DAY OFF

WHEN JOE PEPITONE is in the house, there are three ways to know. Number one—by a long shot—is his "hair," if you can call it that. Actually, it's a Frankie Avalon–style hairpiece glued to his otherwise bald head. The rug adds another five or six inches to his six-foot-plus frame, making him tower above most everyone else. Pep is credited with being the first Major League Baseball player ever to use an electric hair dryer in the clubhouse locker room. Sadly, that may be the defining event of his career.

The second way you know Pep's in the house is, no matter where he goes, he always eats and drinks for free. Everybody in the biz seems to know and accept that Peppy simply doesn't pay. For some reason, Bert Sugar, the noted boxing pundit, doesn't pay either. Together, they are America's guests.

The third way you know Pep's around is that wherever he is, he's talking loudly . . . about himself and his glory days of slamming home runs and nailing groupies. Give Pep a soapbox any night of the week and keep him well lubricated, and he'll spin right on through closing time. Much like his hair, Pep is one of those larger-than-life baseball players.

When Peppy first came up at nineteen as a dimple-chinned, left-handed, power-hitting first baseman from Brooklyn, he crushed a dozen homers in the grapefruit league, breaking Mickey's spring record. With his natural powerhouse swing (made to order for the short porch at the Stadium), Pepitone was a star waiting to be born—and an accident waiting to happen.

Joe's career fell tragically short of expectations. He details his athletic failures in his autobiography, *Joe, You Coulda Made Us Proud.* Lackluster record or no, he romps around as though he invented the game. He's got the kind of moxie Neil Simon refers to in the American classic, *Lost in Yonkers.* In New York, we call it *charismatic chutzpah.*

The first time I met Joe at Mantle's, a sloshed Mickey told a wasted Pepitone to stay away from his table, because he was, as Mick put it, "a fucking embarrassment." Joe furrowed his densely knit brows for a beat before slapping Mick on the back and launching right into another unintelligible story.

Joe's favorite Mickey memory was about the time when he had found Mick in their hotel room at the St. Moritz with his vomit-covered face between the legs of a famous actress (whose name the editor says I can't mention). When asked if he'd gone in for the sloppiest of seconds, Pep just winked and ordered a round of drinks for everyone.

"Salud, everybody, it's on me."

Actually, it was on *me*, but let's not split hairs.

One day, after getting busted, convicted, and briefly imprisoned on Rikers Island for possession of a gym bag full of Quaaludes, Joe was holding court at the bar, explaining to me and everybody around us that he "didn't do it." It seems that on the night of the arrest, Joe's car broke down in Brooklyn, forcing him to hitchhike. Just his luck, the guy who picked him up had a busted headlight, and the cops pulled them over.

"And here's what you're fucking not going to fucking believe," he added. "When they fucking searched the car they found a fucking Yankee gym bag stuffed to the fucking gills with fucking Quaaludes."

He was right about the first part: I didn't "fucking believe" a word of his story, and neither did a dozen other eavesdropping jurists at the bar.

"Joe," I said, "who are you kidding? The bag had your name embroidered on it."

"I *know*," he shrieked, "what a fucking coincidence!" Then he leaned toward me and his voice dropped to a stage whisper. "Bill," he said, "do you really think I would be so fucking stupid as to carry three *thousand* Quaaludes in a fucking gym bag with my fucking *name* on it?"

"No, Joe," I answered, "there's no fucking way you'd do something that stupid."

"You're the best, Bill," he replied. "Hey, everybody: Drinks on me!"

A few years later, Joe stopped by Mickey's around 3:00 p.m. for a couple of free drinks. He ordered a shot of Glenlivet, threw it down, and signaled the barkeep for another.

"What are you up to, Joe?" I asked him, hoping he wasn't in the mood to hang out and "buy" rounds for everyone at the bar.

"Fucking Bill," Peppy said, as he slapped me on the back, way too hard. "No sweat, I just stopped by for a couple of pops after my AA meeting. Now I'm on my way to pick up the old lady from her fucking Al-Anon meeting. Not to worry."

He chugged his second shot of scotch and shot off into the street to complete his evening of personal and family therapy.

22

WHOA, NELLIE!

WHEN PAT RILEY FAXED his resignation to the Knicks, the team was hard-pressed to find a high-profile replacement. Enter Mr. Don Nelson.

The Iowa University product was a hayseed by New York City standards—even after a pro career that boasted several championships with the Celtics and coach-of-the-year awards with both the Milwaukee Bucks and the Golden State Warriors. Don and I had a mutual friend, and whenever the Warriors were in town to play the Knicks or the Nets, Don would drop by Mickey's for a few dozen brewskies. Yet, despite his impressive accolades and frequent sojourns to the city, he was unprepared for the white-light scrutiny of the Big Apple media.

The Knicks called a press conference at Mickey's to introduce him as their new head coach. By some bizarre coincidence, the highly anticipated verdict at the OJ Simpson trial was announced at the exact moment the press conference was about to begin. So between the Knicks entourage and the OJ circus, the place was stuffed to the gills. As the words *not guilty* were pronounced on live television, everything and everyone stopped on a dime, including Nellie's (Nelson's) introduction to the pack of jackals called the New York media. You literally could have heard a pin drop; there's no other way to explain it. For the duration of a single moment, every sports pundit, tourist freeloader, basketball functionary, beer-bellied drunk, and high-priced sex worker at the bar stopped talking and listened to the late-breaking news.

The verdict ignited a thundering chorus of boos, peppered with a few lonely cheers. After the ruckus petered out, the press conference was under way with OJ and Nellie on their minds.

Afterward, Nellie sat for interviews with a couple of local scribes. Standing guard at tableside was Josh, the Knicks' pint-sized press marionette with flaming red hair and a beard to match. Soon, the waiter arrived to take Nelson's drink order.

"Just gimme a Bud Light," he said.

Hearing his order, Josh tapped Nelson on the shoulder and mouthed the words *Diet Coke* in an exaggerated lip-synch.

"On second thought, just gimme a Diet Coke," Nellie said, adjusting his order. Pretty smooth transition, given the fact that if the conference had been in Milwaukee, Nelson and the entire press corps would have been on their third or fourth cold one already.

Fast-forward to the season's opening, when Ewing, Mason, and Starks led New York to a quick 7–3 start. The honeymoon was in full swing, and the knock-knock joke around town was, "Pat *Who?*"

One night, out of the blue, Nellie called me at home. I was sick in bed with a nasty case of the flu, self-medicating with steady doses of marijuana. The grass killed the nausea, but I was still hot, cold, shivering, and whacked out of my head.

"So what do you think of the team?" Nellie asked.

"Great, great," I mumbled, totally unprepared to engage in any sort of adult conversation. I sucked it up and took a shot from way downtown: "Just one suggestion," I said, as my thoughts began to crystallize, "let Anthony Mason handle the ball more often in the post and on the wing. He's got great hands, he's a terrific passer, and we're all so fucking sick and tired of watching the ball get forced into Ewing . . . He either drops the fucking ball or heaves up a fallaway jump shot that only bricks when the game is on the line. I mean, Ewing's like the proverbial black hole—the ball goes in there and it never comes out." I stopped to catch a breath and was shocked to find that Nellie was still on the line and had been listening to my every labored word.

"Okay, thanks Bill. Great idea about Mason. Feel better." The click of the phone indicated the call was over.

The next day, Nellie held an impromptu press conference and announced the following strategic offensive change: Anthony Mason would now be the point-forward, and the offense would go through him. For the first time in his career, Ewing would not be the primary offensive option.

A few days later, I went with Nellie to make an appearance at the children's cancer ward at Sloan-Kettering, where he had been nominated by me to receive the annual Award of Courage. If you can believe it, he wanted to visit all the kids in the ward. My mouth hung open as Nellie exchanged greetings with every child on the ward and spent time chatting them up and putting smiles on their tiny shrunken faces.

"Hi, I'm Don Nelson, coach of the New York Knicks. Do you guys like basketball?" he would ask the pint-sized sports fans and instant new converts in his midst.

Afterward, he dropped me off at Mickey's on the way to coach a game for the 13–5 Knicks.

"Bill," he said, "I thought you told me the New York press was a nightmare. They are a piece of cake," he said, licking his lips.

"Wait until you go on a five-game losing streak," I warned him. We chuckled in unison and I left the car, thanking him for a beautiful and inspirational afternoon.

Several days later, Nelson was fired while in his Philadelphia hotel room. The move was allegedly inspired by a nasty confrontation between Nellie and Ewing and his personal caddy John Starks—both of whom bitched about Ewing's new and diminished role in the offense, or lack thereof. Nelson was replaced by Jeff Van Gundy, who just so happens to be a good buddy of Patrick's. (After he retired, Ewing went on to serve as an assistant coach under Van Gundy with the Houston Rockets.)

Nelson was sacked on a Saturday and was scheduled to accept his Award of Courage from Sloan-Kettering on the following Thursday. He went undercover and tried to get his head around being fired with a winning record. For four days, he shunned the press in order to collect his thoughts. He called me on Monday.

"Bill," he said, "now that they canned me, I guess you want to give that award to someone else."

"Are you kidding me?" I said. "We absolutely, 100 percent want you."

"Oh . . . Okay," he replied, in barely more than a whisper. His response was understated, but I could tell he was deeply touched. "I'm not going to talk to the press until then."

Luckily, our charity event turned into a media circus, but Nellie conducted himself with untarnished class and perfect finesse, declining to bad-mouth the participants in the palace coup. During the party that followed, Nellie pulled me aside to tell me what really happened.

"All I can tell you is this," he revealed. "In my half-century of playing and coaching basketball, I have never had a bigger, more selfish asshole on my team than Patrick Ewing."

The next day, Nellie hobbled onto a plane bound for his off-season Shangri-La in Maui, pocketing the remaining money on his guaranteed five-year, multimillion-dollar contract.

Nellie returned to the mainland to coach perennial playoff contender Dallas Mavericks for five outstanding seasons. After taking a year off pounding ice-cold Bud Lights in Hawaii, he recently signed to return to the Golden State Warriors, a three-point-shot from his spread in the Bay Area.

During his previous tenure with the Warriors, Nellie coached the Rum TMC Team with: *T*, Tim Hardaway (22.9 ppg); *M*, Mitch Richmond (23.9 ppg); and *C*, Chris Mullin (25.7 ppg).

In 1990, Nelson amused himself and the basketball community by posting seven-foot, six-inch Manute Bol outside to take forty-eight three-point shots. (He made nine.)

23

LAWSUITS RESTAURANT STYLE

In the United States, we see many frivolous lawsuits—the ones where 33 percent of the winnings go to the ambulance chaser and the plaintiff has nothing to lose as long as he or she can find a lawyer willing to take the case on contingency. In the UK, it's a different story. The loser pays all the legal fees for both sides, which makes people think twice before tossing around Hail Mary lawsuits. President Bush is currently pushing new legislation to limit the amount of money a jury can award in a personal injury case. Much as I think the guy is the village idiot, I actually agree with him on this issue. When a plaintiff gets $500,000 for spilling a cup of scalding hot McDonald's coffee on her own lap, you know things have gotten out of hand.

Mantle's has been hit with dozens of horseshit lawsuits. All of them got settled out of court by our insurance company. Since settling out of court is the status quo these days, any halfway decent grifter can pretty much have his way with the system.

Suit 1: Murder at Mickey's

It was a cold December night in 1992. The restaurant was percolating with holiday traffic when a tall, spindly woman in her thirties pushed her way through the revolving door. She went straight to the manager and explained that her husband was outside in a wheelchair and would we please avail him of a wheelchair-accessible entrance. The manager led the two of them through the side entrance into the dining room's lower level.

"This won't do," the woman objected. "We don't want to sit in Siberia. We want to be part of the action."

As I eyed her invalid husband nodding off in his wheelchair, I had my doubts. He hardly looked like he wanted to be schlepped up five steps and wedged into the heart of a teeming, tourist-packed dining room with a loud Knicks game providing the background noise. "Seat us up there," she insisted, "near the bar."

Since the customer is always right, we rustled up two bussers and a runner to help hoist the guy up the stairs in his steel-and-titanium throne. We're talking about upward of 300 pounds, so the maneuver was less than graceful. Customers looked on anxiously from their tables.

After a lot of heaving and grunting, we reached the top alive. The manager seated the mister and missus at a table of the lady's choosing. Now she turned her negative attention away from the staff and refocused it onto her ironsided groom, dissing and dressing him down during dinner.

"You're the blight of my life," she told him.

Ironsides seemed to take it all in stride—apparently, he'd been down this road before.

When the enchanted evening was over, she paid the check and hastily wheeled her husband toward the stairs without alerting anyone for assistance. The same porters and waiters who had toted him up the stairs jockeyed for position to reverse the procedure.

"Hands off," she snapped. "I don't need your help. It's not as though you did such a great job on the way up." Then, before anyone could intervene, she grabbed the wheelchair by its handles, reared back for momentum, and shoved her husband down the stairs face-first. Think Nordberg.

It gets worse. She hadn't bothered to fasten his safety belt, so as the chair plummeted down the steps like a massive iron slinky, its passenger bounced right out of it and landed in a dreadful-looking heap at the bottom.

The searing gasp throughout the restaurant could have busted some sonic eardrum. It was one of those truly cinematic moments wherein slow motion engulfs the scene and all you can hear through the vortex of your disbelief is a collective, baritone *Nooooo*. Like Darth Vader on 'ludes or something.

"Morons," wailed the wife, "what are you trying to do, kill him? You just stand idly by and watch my husband break his ass on a flight of stairs?"

She and the manager propped the tubby hubby upright. To everyone's relief, the old man was still breathing.

"Are you all right, sir?" everyone demanded at once.

"Fine," he answered, "just give me a double shot of Johnny Walker Black—neat—and we'll be on our way."

This seemed like very little to ask in recompense for his troubles, and so we naturally obliged him instantly. We probably would have given him the bottle to take home if he'd asked.

He heartily downed the drink, and she rolled him out onto Central Park South without incident.

A week later, the lawsuit arrived. Tragically, it turns out that

Ironsides had died in his sleep the night of his fall, due to a blood clot originating from his leg. The suit contended that the clot had come from the fall, which had been caused by "negligent and reckless behavior" on the part of the staff. As such, the wife demanded ten million in pain, suffering, loss, and damages. This suit, if successful, would far exceeded our five-million-dollar umbrella policy, and would have put our lights out faster than you could sing, *Turn out the lights, the party's over.*

Luckily, the insurance company provides the first line of defense in these legal dustups. After reviewing the actuary charts, they concluded that we ought to settle this one out of court rather than risking years of mounting litigation fees and the outside possibility of a huge, John Edwards–style award in open court. They settled the case for $100,000 cash to the Black Widow, which resulted in a hefty increase to our annual coverage rate. In the final analysis, wifey got paid a hundred grand for offing her husband.

Suit 2: Rubber Band Man

I hired a steward named Jack to lower our food cost and improve the quality of our ingredients. Jack came from the food service department of Madison Square Garden with glowing recommendations. According to his resumé he "changed the culture at the Garden" and "chopped food cost by 10 percent." On our food purchase of over one million dollars a year, that would mean a net savings of one hundred thousand dollars. I hired him on the spot.

It turned out to mean that he purchased inferior products at the same price and pocketed the difference off the top. It's called a kickback, or "points and onions" in the trade. But who knew? The resumé made no mention of it.

Jack's resumé also failed to mention his compulsive gambling and the bottle of brown liquid he kept in his desk drawer for easy access. He had a code name—"Mr. Lucky"—that he used to identify himself to the bookie on the phone.

"Yes, hello, this is Mr. Lucky," he could often be heard in a loud whisper from behind his office door. "Gimme a dime on Georgia Tech, *now.* Kickoff's in two minutes!"

Mr. Lucky spent most of his time at the office in this manner, placing bets and nursing moonshine to ease the pain of his mounting losses. As for his effects on our food costs at Mantle's, we could have called him Mr. Unlucky. He chose his purveyors based on the size of the kickbacks. He was able to provide us with low-grade burger patties priced like filet mignon.

I came into work early one morning. It happened to be the end of the month: inventory day. Jack was behind the bar, drinking directly from a bottle of Jack Daniels. Between swigs, he marked the inventory nonchalantly on a bar napkin. Great system. I played dumb and shot past him down to the office, but I was hopping mad and thinking about revenge.

Around lunchtime, Jack emerged from his office to order a bowl of linguini with tomato sauce. Ten minutes later, I saw his food sitting on the slide. I grabbed a double fistful of rubber bands from the service station and heaped them onto the pasta, swirling them around in the sauce for camouflage. As an afterthought, I dropped a couple of extra bands right on top for garnish and topped it off with a sprig of basil. Then I loitered around the kitchen a few minutes to make sure it didn't fall into the wrong hands. Jack returned for his pasta and whisked it back downstairs.

It wasn't long before Jack came after me, and he was pretty pissed off.

"You cocksucker," he bleated, "you ruined my lunch."

"Come on, Jack," I said, "don't tell me you actually ate one of those rubber bands."

I never should have said it, because I believe it was at that moment Jack figured this could be Mr. Lucky's lucky day.

His next phone call was to his lawyer, who advised him to swallow exactly one rubber band, hightail it to the emergency room for X-rays, and prepare to own Mickey Mantle's outright.

Now let's get real: rubber bands taste like dirty socks. I know this because I touched one with the tip of my tongue. The smell alone would make a starving goat steer clear. How a single office rubber band got past this man's nose and into his mouth . . . well, you get the point. It just didn't happen by accident.

After downing the rubber, Jack raced into my office looking supremely satisfied with himself.

"I almost choked, you fuckers," he said, coughing several times for emphasis. "I'm going to St. Luke's to have this thing pumped out of my stomach . . . before I *die*."

Three days later, Jack returned to work. His arrival was followed by the service of a five-million-dollar lawsuit. Well, I thought, if he was suing me, I was firing him.

It didn't go down so easy. At eight o'clock in the morning, his breath already smelled like half booze and half crème de menthe. "Look, Jack," I said at one point, "it was just a practical joke. Drop the suit, keep your job. Let's smoke the peace pipe and move on."

What I was really thinking was that I would fire him another way on another day, after this whole mess had blown over.

"There is no way I'm dropping the suit," he insisted. "You tried to kill me, and you almost got away with it. You're lucky I don't press criminal charges."

"I didn't mean for you to actually eat the rubber bands," I told him. "I thought you'd spit them out."

"Tell it to the judge," he grouched, and stumbled out the door.

The next day a stack of legal documents arrived, complete with X-rays of his stomach featuring the lonely rubber band looking like a neon tapeworm eating its own tail. A note from Jack's lawyer demanded his job back with a sizable raise and a $100,000 cash settlement if we wanted to stay out of court.

As far as I knew, we had no practical joke insurance in our portfolio, and Shechtman advised me to settle. After weeks of haggling, Mr. Lucky settled for ten grand. We agreed that he would not get his job back, but that I would be obliged to write a glowing recommendation for him to brandish in front of prospective employers.

> *To Whom It May Concern:*
> *Jack is a man of the highest integrity. His knowledge of the food-service industry is unsurpassed in my experience of twenty-five years in the business. He is as honest as the day is long, gets along well with his peers, takes direction, always comes to work promptly, and stays long after quitting time He would be an asset to any organization, and, if given the chance, I would not hesitate to hire him back. Mickey Mantle's is far better off now that Jack has lent his expertise to our food-service operation. If there are any other questions I can answer about this saint of a man, please do not hesitate to contact me.*
> *Sincerely,*
> *William Liederman, Proprietor*

So, while the Black Widow got a hundred grand for pushing her husband to his doom, Mr. Lucky took home a $10,000 bonus for eating a rubber band. Hell, for ten grand, I'd swallow a roll of packing tape.

Suit 3: Flash Flood

One evening a male-female tag team of shysters reigned terror on the ladies rest room. The woman went inside and cupped her hands under the faucet, spattering the floor with torrents of water. Once a puddle had formed, she spread-eagled herself on the tiles and began to wail for help. The woman claimed she couldn't move, so the manger called an ambulance to whisk Bonnie and Clyde away to the ER. She was fine but managed to get some quack MD to say that she had suffered "lifestyle-altering" back injuries, and she wrung another $10,000 out of the insurance company. Ladies and gentlemen, would you lie on a wet bathroom floor for ten grand? If not, let that be God's way of telling you that you have too much money.

Suit 4: The Seven-Martini Lunch

A guest of the St. Moritz Hotel came into Mickey's one time and knocked off seven martinis over the course of a two-hour stay at the bar. Our bartender turned a blind eye to the excess, not wanting to blow his growing gratuity.

After the seventh round, martini-man got in touch with his inner gay self and picked up another man at the bar. The two of them went back to the St. Moritz together, presumably to make whoopie. Hours later, the seven-martini man left the hotel for some air, tried to cross the street against the light, and got hit by a cab. He sustained only mild injuries, but when I received his legal missive, the medical jargon to describe what amounts to a sprained knee went on for three pages: arterial, material, meniscus, hibiscus of the discus, and all the rest. Nobody knew what he'd consumed between lunch and the time of the accident, but that hardly mattered. The insurance company settled the case for a cool $20,000.

Suit 5: Bubby Made a Kishke

A young Jewish woman came in to apply for a hostess position. During the interview, the manager made the mistake of asking what religion she was. It was a stupid question, but he only asked because Yom Kippur and Rosh Hashanah were approaching, and he wanted to know if she'd be available to work those days. She said no problem, and so we scheduled her for the upcoming week.

On her first day of work, she went home early with an upset stomach. Then she pulled a no-show on her next five shifts and failed to return any calls. We took this as a resignation and went with someone else.

The following Monday, she showed up ready to work. The baffled manager explained that she'd been replaced, and she stormed out the door.

Months later, we got served by the Department of Employment for violating New York State's antidiscrimination law. The documents stipulated that we'd fired the no-show hostess because she was Jewish, thereby violating her civil rights. Thankfully, her claim was denied, maybe in part because I am Jewish!

Suit 6: Cutting-Room Floor

Several years ago a woman came in during a World Series game. As she staggered up to the bar, wobbling like an eighteen-wheeler on nine wheels, it was clear that she'd had quite enough to drink. The bartender refused to serve her and she settled for a glass of water, which she promptly dropped on the floor. Then she whirled around and slipped in the puddle she had made, fell on the glass, and cut her hand. The manager bandaged the tiny boo-boo, then helped the woman into a cab and gave her twenty bucks to pay the driver.

I was sure a lawsuit was forthcoming, and I was right. According to the legal briefs, she had not only been "gouged," but had suffered "back injuries, emotional stress, loss of livelihood," and every other ailment under the sun. This case was settled for $10,000.

Suit 7: Legends of the Fall

The final case on today's legal docket involves an employee of 40 Central Park South, the building in which Mantle's is housed. According to him and his lawyer, he slipped and fell down some stairs in the restaurant's basement. Never mind that he was *not* employed by Mantle's and had no business being there in the first place. Never mind that the fall allegedly took place after hours and nobody was around to see, hear, or witness it in any way.

After three years of depositions, the intruder won an undisclosed settlement from our insurance company, all for creepin' round my backstairs.

My advice to those considering a career in the restaurant business: Don't bother. Go to law school and then become a personal injury lawyer. That's where the real money is.

24

MTC VERSUS NHL

THE MANHATTAN THEATER CLUB (MTC) had just opened a play written by Terrence McNally at the City Center, on 55th Street, a few blocks away from Mickey's. The opening night party at Mantle's was booked well in advance, with the cast, crew, and over two hundred well-wishers slated to attend. It was an 8:00 p.m. curtain, so the guests were due to land at Mickey's somewhere around 10:30.

This was the same evening that everyone in Mickey's was watching game four of the NHL finals, pitting the New York Rangers against the Vancouver Canucks. They dropped the puck at 7:00, so the game should have been over by 10:00 at the *latest*, leaving just enough time to flip the room for the next event. Nobody could have imagined that the game would go into *triple* overtime, throwing inebriated, brain-dead hockey fans and snooty thespians alike into a single, churning crucible of ungainly coexistence.

By 10:45, Mantle's was a motley hodgepodge of macho hockey fanatics in Messier jerseys and flamboyant, Pucci-clad playwrights.

I had no idea what to do. The Ranger fans had been glued to their seats for almost four hours, stuffing their faces with chicken-friend steak and bathing their livers in briny adult beverages. These do-or-die Ranger fans had hunkered down, and they weren't going to unhunker until somebody scored a goal.

The MTC patrons quickly grew impatient. They looked down the shafts of their plastic schnozzes at the hockey goons, who snarled right back at them. The full attention of the fans was bent on the game, which flashed endlessly across the wide-screen TVs and reverberated from the speakers. The fans howled, the theatergoers cringed. I tried to get the hockey people out of their seats.

I mentioned my dilemma to the hockey crowd, but they didn't go for it.

"Fuck you, asshole," one of them bellowed. "I just dropped three hundred bucks in this place and I ain't budging from this seat until the FUCKING hockey game is OVER," he yelled, giving the table a mighty tomahawk chop.

I could see a major shit storm gathering on the horizon. I had unwittingly double-booked the place to these thugs and Ron Shechtman's wife, Lynne Meadow, artistic director of the MTC, whom I wanted to impress.

For twenty minutes and throughout the second overtime, the battle waged on: Rangers versus Canucks on the ice, hockey fans versus theatergoers in the restaurant. My brain was screaming. I prayed for a goal by either team: *Shot . . . save* and *shot . . . hits the post,* followed by, *shot . . . wide, the Rangers ice the puck.*

Late into the third overtime, the actors began arriving at the MTC party. Finally, I heard some very sweet music: *SCORE!* The

Rangers had won. Within minutes, the hockey hooligans quickly drained out of the restaurant, leaving a trail of unpaid checks.

The theater party began forty-five minutes behind schedule. Despite my "in" with Lynne Meadow, it was the last time MTC booked a party at Mantle's.

25

SLICK AND SLICKER

OVER THE YEARS AT Mickey Mantle's, I have had the pleasure of meeting a bunch of really nice ballplayers, many of whom were personally introduced to me by Mickey. However, there was one good ol' boy for whom I developed a keen distaste. His name was Whitey "Slick" Ford.

I met Whitey my first year at the Mickey Mantle/Whitey Ford Fantasy Baseball Camp in Florida. Mickey invited me down to be a camper, on him—as long as I promised not to tell Whitey. Despite my delicious BMOC status as Mickey's partner, I could feel a chill in the air every time Whitey and I were within tobacky-spittin' distance. At first I wasn't sure why, but I guessed it had something to do with my being comped. In short, he saw me as a freeloading, deadbeat tagalong, and he couldn't hide his contempt.

Coincidentally, I had gone to high school with one of Whitey's sons, Eddie Ford. Eddie was a superjock who excelled in football and basketball and was a lights-out pitcher on the baseball team. I had more important things to do, such as marching against the war in Vietnam, raising money for the starving children of Biafra, and chasing all the hippie chicks at school. We never actually met at school, but now, Eddie and his brother Tommy were at camp that year to serve as permanent catchers.

The next year, I couldn't ask Mickey for another freebie, and couldn't afford the $4,000 tuition, so I took a Pasadena. The day before camp was scheduled to start, Mickey called me from the manager's office in the Ft. Lauderdale clubhouse—the same office that had housed legendary Yankee managers such as Casey Stengel, Ralph Houk, Billy Martin, and Yogi Berra.

"Yo, pard," he trumpeted, "we need a catcher. Jump on a plane and get your fat ass down here!"

I had a full week of work, family, and social plans ahead, but I canceled everything and did as I was told by Mickey. This was my first professional baseball contract. Instead of being a paying camper, I was actually going to be paid to play alongside a gaggle of Yankee greats. *I'm getting paid to play baseball,* I said to anyone who would listen.

I arrived in Ft. Lauderdale just in time for that morning's scheduled doubleheader. Mickey was waiting for me in the locker room. "Strap that shit on," he said, pointing to the tools of ignorance, "and haul ass over to field two, *now.*"

I speed-suited up and dashed to the field. My catcher's vest was inside out and my shin-guard buckles were askew. I knew I looked like a novice, but I didn't have time to fix it. On my way out of the clubhouse, I bumped into Whitey.

"Liederman," he snarled, "what the fuck are you doing here? I didn't see you on the list of paid campers! Get the fuck out of my catcher's gear and go back to run Mickey's restaurant."

Even in the context of locker-room tough talk, this really hurt. For the first time since I struck out looking at a bad pitch to end the Little League season, I almost burst into tears.

"Mickey invited me to come down and catch," I offered feebly.

"Bullshit. Mickey never told me that and besides," he added, "you can't catch for shit, and you throw like a girl."

Just then Mickey sauntered out of the skipper's office.

"Slick," he asked, "what's up?"

"Liederman wants another freebie . . . No pay, no play," Whitey blurted. "Over my fucking dead body he plays without paying."

"Cool down, Slick," Mickey said. "I hired him. Since your boys couldn't make it this year, we needed a catcher, and ol' Bill here can do the job."

For the next several years, I was a regular catcher at the camp, and Whitey avoided me like the clap. During that time, Mickey's lawyer, Roy True, conducted a forensic audit of the camp's financial records. Roy couldn't figure out why Mickey's cut of the pie was so skinny while the camp was raking in the big tuition bucks. Mickey told me that the accounting indicated Whitey had allegedly charged some of his personal expenses to the camp, all but obliterating the bottom line.

Mickey never cared about money as long as he had a wad of twenties in his pocket. To him, camp was a chance to bond with his sons, see his girlfriend, get a little sunshine, and catch up with his old Yankee pals, including Moose, Blanch, and Hank.

Mickey and Whitey had always called each other "Slick." Mickey dubbed Whitey first, because he was a city slicker in Mickey's estimation. Whitey followed suit and flipped it around on Mickey, a straw-suitcase-carrying country boy. Kind of like calling a fat man "Slim." Now, for the first time, the name Slick took on a whole new meaning.

When Mickey learned of Whitey's less orthodox expenses, he was crushed. Along with Billy Martin, Whitey had been his best friend in the world. The rift was irrevocable. The next year, there were two fantasy baseball camps in Ft. Lauderdale: The Mickey Mantle Fantasy Baseball Camp and The Whitey Ford Fantasy Baseball Camp the week after.

Whitey's camp lasted only a few seasons before wilting, but Mickey's camp thrives to this very day. It is now known as Heroes in Pinstripes and is operated by his pals, Hank and Moose. At age fifty-four, I am still invited down each year to catch, and of course, to be with Hank and Moose and the rest of the guys. Whitey is and always will be persona non grata.

The next time I saw Whitey, he was making an appearance for a pharmaceutical company at Mantle's. We avoided each other, but by happenstance, we collided as he was leaving.

"Liederman," he said, "I need some help promoting my new book. You're a good promoter. Can you line me up some interviews with book reviewer types?"

Mistaking this overture for an extended olive branch, I took down a few notes about the book and said I'd see what I could do. Whitey gave me his home phone number in Lake Success and told me to call him as soon as I had any nibbles.

The next day, I contacted a sportswriter pal, Ira Berkow, from *The New York Times* about Whitey's new book. Afterward, I called Whitey to tell him that Berkow would call him.

"Who the fuck is this?" Whitey barked in lieu of the more traditional hello.

"Whitey, Bill Liederman here, from Mickey Mantle's Restaurant."

"You fucking cocksucker," he wailed, "I thought I told you never to call me at home!"

"Uh . . . no," I protested. "You gave me this number and told me to call you as soon as . . ."

"The hell I did," he screamed. "Why the fuck would I do that?"

"I thought you wanted me to help you with your book," I said.

"I don't need your fucking help," he roared, and hung up.

My final sorry story about Mr. Ford involves two of the nicest and friendliest ex-ballplayers you would ever want to meet: Ed Kranepool and Art Shamsky. These guys stayed in the New York area after their careers were over and they are always available to make an appearance for a modest fee—or for no fee, if a charity's involved. Kranepool once owned a restaurant on Long Island and ended up in the convention display business. Shamsky had opened a restaurant with Ron Darling, who was coming off his championship season with the Mets. Darling, a Yale graduate, nixed the name Darling & Shamsky because he thought it was too overstated. Instead they went with the address—17 Murray Street—a name that gave no one the slightest clue who the owners were or what kind of restaurant it was, and it died an early death.

Whitey is notorious for holding up event planners on the eve of an event for more money than they originally bargained for, sometimes demanding double his original fee. Once he arrives at an event, Whitey will drink too many vodka tonics, get surly, and then be too drunk to give a speech.

Kranepool made no mystery of the low regard in which he held Whitey. I had the honor of sitting next to him and Shamsky at a BAT dinner. The Baseball Assistance Team is an organization that raises money for retired ballplayers who are down on their luck. Despite the opulent contracts of today's pro athletes, players from

Mickey's era had little or no pensions; some of them were even living in their cars. Ed had just had "Tommy John" surgery on his arm—not to make a comeback, but to be able to lift his grandchildren. I became his designated food cutter.

"Whitey Ford's a cocksucker," he hissed, as I sawed his leathery sirloin into bite-sized cubes.

"How so?" I asked.

"A couple of weeks ago, I got a call from the Mohegan Sun. They needed some players to appear at an event they were having. They said their budget was $10,000 plus expenses for the two players, so I called Shamsky up and we made the deal. A few days later, the casino booker calls me back and asks me to book Whitey, so I put Whitey in touch with the casino guy. I warned the guy that Whitey's fee was usually in the range of ten grand."

A few days went by, and Whitey called Kranepool. "Bad news Krane," he announced, "they canceled the event."

Kranepool told me he was a bit disappointed, but he soon forgot about it. A week later Kranepool saw an item in the paper about Whitey's appearance at the Mohegan Sun.

It turns out that the Slickster had allegedly demanded $20,000 for the appearance. This doubled their original fee and left Krane and Shamsky sitting on the bench. Krane paraphrased for me what Slick supposedly said to the suits at the casino: "Who the fuck needs those guys? Make a choice, either pay me the full twenty, or I'm not showing up. Don't worry; I'll smooth things over with Sham and Krane."

Whitey is a very wealthy man, not so much from his glorious tenure with the Yankees, but more so from fantasy camp, autographs, appearances, and some Baskin-Robbins ice cream parlors he opened on Long Island. No need to throw a rent party for the chairman of the board.

Deliciously so, Whitey opened a Whitey Ford's restaurant in the parking lot of the Roosevelt Field shopping mall on Long Island. I drove past it once and noticed that the logo and the interior decor were carbon copied off of Mickey Mantle's in New York. A few months later, Whitey's was gone.

26

BELLY-UP

As MANTLE'S ROLLED into its fourteenth season, with a gaggle of new kids and the mounting expense of living in Manhattan, my finances were painted the color red. We lived paycheck to paycheck in our Central Park South apartment above the store, which a ludicrous 125 percent of my income went toward. Talk about *apartment poor*, we were *apartment piss-poor*. When my third child, Emmy, arrived, I decided it was finally time to pull the trigger on a second Mickey Mantle's.

For years, people had been hounding me about opening a second Mantle outpost and then expanding into other cities, eventually going public and off to the Restaurant Hall of Fame. When Mickey was alive, I would gingerly approach him with questions about his possible interest in opening a second spot.

"Hey, Mick," I would say, "I know some guys who want us to open a Mantle's in Cleveland . . ."

"Ah hate Cleveland," he'd answer.

"Detroit?"

"Fuck Detroit."

"Baltimore?"

"Baltimore sucks."

"Well, what doesn't suck?"

"Dallas."

Oddly enough, Dallas is the worst possible city for a baseball theme restaurant, because it is a football town with a capital F. I had noticed, on several trips to Dallas with Mickey, that he was scarcely recognized at all. Maybe that's why he liked the place.

Over the years, I had received many inquiries about a Mantle's franchise in various locations around the New York area as well as such urban utopias as Detroit, Chicago, Philadelphia, Washington, Fort Lauderdale, Los Angeles, and even Tokyo.

When it came to new restaurant proposals, I had a standard pitch: "If you have a great location, a strong background in the restaurant business, enough money to build and operate successfully, and you are prepared to pay us a royalty, then we can talk."

Despite a lot of initial enthusiasm, no group ever met these requirements. Along the way, I received two key pieces of advice. The first came from my daughter Chloe when she was just eight years old: "Daddy," she said, "don't open up another Mickey Mantle's. This is a one-of-a-kind place. It's very special and it is very *you*. Besides, you'd be away so much that I would never see you again." Out of the mouths of babes . . .

The second piece of advice came from Frankie Guido, the owner of Mariner's Harbor Restaurant in the Hudson Valley. When Frankie came to Mickey's on a busman's holiday, he spread the love—handing out Ben Franklins to any restaurant employee he came in contact with.

Frankie pounded drinks, slapped palms, and thumped backs from the moment he arrived until he crawled into his limo for the ride home. He spoke with the furry-tongued drawl of a drunken Joe Pesci, but his advice to me was simple: "Hey Bill, don't be a fuggin' idiot. If you open another joint, you risk losing 'em both. Instead of spreading yourself thinner than fuggin' Creeps Suzettes, just work harder and pay more fuggin' attention to the joint and make an additional 10 fuggin' percent on the bottom line. Think of Mariner's Harbor," he said. "I had three or four of these cock-sucking places, and it almost killed me. I wound up wit less dough and five times the aggravation. Don't be a fuggin' idiot, you fuggin' idiot. Feel me, bro?"

I felt him, alright. I felt him because his hands were all over my arms and back, loving me up.

Despite his brilliant advice, after Emmy arrived in this world, and the occupancy costs at the restaurant went up, up, and away, I knew it was time for Mantle's II. I set off in search of a second location within a forty-five-minute drive from midtown Manhattan. After a couple of months of fruitless searching, Tom Valenti of Pyramid Leasing came to visit me at Mantle's. He had some restaurant space left in the new Palisades Center in West Nyack, which already had Dave & Busters, Friday's, Chili's, Outback Steakhouse, Legal Seafood, Johnny Rocket's, and some bottom-feeding Mexican place with a name like Nacho Mamas.

"So you want me to put a Mantle's in your mall?" I asked.

"It's not a mall," he corrected me sternly. "It's The Palisades *Center*," he said, as though there were a world of difference.

He was the smoothest talker east of Bill Clinton. He flattered me with his love of Mickey and the restaurant. He sent a limo for us on our first trip to the mall—I mean *Center*—and led us though the proposed space as though we were visiting dignitaries. The next week, I was in the area with my wife and I asked her opinion.

"I don't know, Bill," she said. "Mickey Mantle's is an up-market concept. This mall is low-rent."

"It's not a mall; it's a *Center*," I explained.

In my gut I agreed with her logic, but I charged ahead with the deal, telling myself that because all the other restaurants in the mall were doing telephone-book numbers, Mickey's could actually hit the green pages.

I rounded up a group of local investors, and together we built a 25,000-square-foot version of the original Mantle's in the Center. There were crippling construction delays, and the partners insisted on opening prematurely, right smack dab in the middle of the holiday season—even though the staff hadn't been trained yet. My partners, virgins in the restaurant business and eager to stop the financial hemorraghing, filled all 245 seats in twenty minutes. This was like committing restaurant hari-kari. The servers, bussers, and cooks were not ready to serve half that number of people, as many of them had been hired the same day. Initial word-of-mouth was god-awful and the restaurant hung on for just over a year until the local utility company pulled the plug.

The fallout was disastrous. I had been the schmuck with the pen and signed personally for $75,000 worth of restaurant equipment, all of which was eventually auctioned off for minus-ten cents on the dollar.

After this shit storm settled, I had no choice but to declare personal bankruptcy, a move that would ultimately cost me my ownership of Mantle's. The Nyack location had opened just a month after 9/11 and Mantle's NYC was also choked with debt. I spent the month sifting through a pile of chapter-eleven applications as high as a Georgia pine and taking phone calls from debt collectors, lawyers, and ex-Nyack employees who still hadn't been paid.

I developed a coping strategy for dealing with the creditors' constant calls.

"Hello," they would chirp, "is this Mr. Liederman?"

"Who wants to know?"

"Imperial Leasing wants to know if you've any intention of paying your bills."

"Every intention, but I can't do it now because I don't have any money."

"Well, Mr. Liederman, when you contracted for these goods and services, did you intend to pay for them?"

"No, of course not. I planned all along to tank the restaurant and stiff every vendor, including your bank."

"Mr. Liederman, you know very well that we will eventually collect the money even if we have to take your house and car."

"That's great. I don't have a house, and the repo man got my car."

"Okay, then how about we work out a payment plan that you can afford? I'll be happy to take a check by phone."

"First of all, I don't have any checks, because all my bank accounts have been frozen. Second of all, what I can afford is zero dollars a month. Take it or leave it."

"This is not a joke, Mr. Liederman. You could be indicted for fraud. How about $5,000 a month?"

"How about no?"

"How about $2,000 a month?"

"Try again."

"$1,000?"

"Still about $1,000 too much."

"Okay, then, Mr. Liederman, what can you afford?"

"Maybe a hundred a month."

"That's not going to work. You owe the bank $39,000. Even with a life expectancy of eighty-five, you'd be dead for fifty years before you'd make good on your debt."

"Well, that's the best I can do."

"Okay, then, we'll see you in court."

"I can't wait."

"Mr. Liederman, why are you being sarcastic with me?"

"Because, you bottom-feeder, if you had half a brain, you would be doing something else with your life instead of vulturing around my soon-to-be-dead body. Maybe something like a bathroom attendant would suit you."

"I don't have to listen to this, Mr. Liederman."

"So don't listen, you Dick-wad."

"I don't think I said anything to warrant that type of comment."

"I can't afford to feed my kids. What part of that don't you understand?"

"Perhaps you should have thought about that in the first place."

"You should have thought about removing your head from your ass before you went to work today."

"Very well, Mr. Liederman, how about $200 a month? If you can afford $100, then I'm sure you can afford $200."

"Maybe, if only my kids could handle going to bed hungry every night."

"You live in a fancy apartment on Central Park South. Surely if you can afford the rent on that place, you can afford $200 a month."

"No, because my next priority after feeding my kids is to keep a roof over their heads."

"It doesn't say on your credit application that you're a comedian. This is your last chance. Either give me a check by phone in the amount of $400 for the first and last payments, or we will call the authorities to your front door, and they will arrest you in front of your wife and kids."

I had become fairly well-versed in debtor's rights, and I knew that the first no-no for collection agents is to threaten the debtor with arrest. In fact, as long as debtors don't understate their income or cheat on their tax returns, they cannot be incarcerated for their debt. I mean, shit, this isn't medieval England.

"You just broke the law, butt munch."

"Look, Mr. Liederman, we're having a reasonable discussion. There's no need for you to use inflammatory language . . . We're coming to the end of our conversation, Mr. Liederman. Are you going to give me a payment by check?"

"Don't interrupt, I'm not finished. It is against the law for you to threaten me with arrest. You could lose your job, and, in fact, you *will* lose your job, as I have tape-recorded this entire conversation."

The debt collector hung up and moved on to the next rotting carcass.

A final note to all my brothers in bankruptcy, especially those in the restaurant biz who got burned through no fault of their own: get to know your debtor's rights. The other thing they can't do is get you on the phone under false pretenses.

Several times, my wife answered the phone and handed it over to me.

"It's an old friend of yours," she said.

"Hello, Mr. Liederman, how are you doing this morning?"

"If I were feeling any better, it would be a crime. What the fuck do you want?"

"I'm with National Finance, and I was hoping we could have a preliminary conversation about the money you owe the bank."

"Well, then I guess nobody told you that according to the debtor's rights manifesto, if you are calling to collect funds, it is illegal to lure the debtor onto the phone under false pretenses. You are required by law to state your purpose from the outset, and failure to do so could get you fired. In fact, you *will* be fired, because I've been taping this entire phone call."

Click.

Finally, I wised up and switched to an unlisted phone number. (An action junkie, I soon began craving these calls.) At work, I screened my phone calls with the utmost care. It didn't always work. Oftentimes, I would check my voice mail and find a message like this: "Good morning, Mr. Liederman, this is Mrs. Jones. I have a very urgent matter that requires your immediate attention. Please call me as soon as possible."

Sometimes, when I needed a little comic relief, I would actually call back.

"Hello, this is Bill Liederman. I'm returning an urgent message. Please don't tell me that my wife and kids have all been killed in a fiery plane crash . . ."

"No, Mr. Liederman, nothing like that. This is Mrs. Jones from Acme Collections. We're currently representing Anheuser-Busch and we're trying to collect the money you owe us for the beer they delivered to your restaurant in West Nyack."

"*Wow,*" I would gasp, "that sounds like a real emergency. If I don't pay you now, the folks at AB will show $3,000 less profit this year, thereby lowering their pretax profit to a measly three billion bucks. Why didn't you call me sooner?"

"There's no need for sarcasm, Mr. Liederman. Don't you want to meet your obligation?"

"It is not my obligation. It's the restaurant's obligation—and the restaurant has been closed for six months."

"Well then, my next call will have to be to the district attorney so that he can send an officer to your door and arrest you in front of your family."

By this time, she had broken two major rules from the debtor's manifesto. She had lied about the purpose of her call, and she had threatened to arrest me.

"Go ahead and make that phone call. *My* next phone call will be to my lawyer to get you fired."

"You're the one who's going to lose your job, not me, Mr. Lie-derman."

"Not really, because I've tape-recorded this entire conversation." Click.

Postscript: One good thing rose from the ashes of the Nyack loca-tion. His name is Maury Allen, and he was the silver lining behind the dark cloud of mall mayhem. When I was growing up in Prince-ton, my mother would come home from trips to "the city" bearing a copy of the *Post*. I would risk life and limb in order to beat my brother to it and read the sports column headed with Maury's pic-ture. Now, years later, he had the bright idea to do a Monday-night radio show live from the Nyack restaurant. Out of that brainstorm, the *Bill & Maury Show* was born, along with my first book, *Our Mickey,* which I coauthored with Maury.

27

THE HOAX OF TED WILLIAMS

THE DIFFERENCE BETWEEN Yankee and Red Sox fans isn't difficult to pinpoint. Until the fall of 2004, the Yanks had won twenty-six World Series titles since 1918, and the Sox hadn't won any. Over time, this chasm between glory and failure has spawned a rivalry of Hatfield-McCoy proportions. I'm talking Montague versus Capulet, Jets versus Sharks, Mailman versus Dog, and the like.

As the male peacock flaunts his fine plumage during mating season, the indigenous Yankee fan bears a breezy confidence during summer months, as the World Series draws steadily closer. The Red Sox fan is markedly less whimsical, as he or she expects not only to lose, but to lose in some spectacular manner, in some terrible blaze of botched glory.

Ron Shechtman's, a fanatical Red Sox fan, idea of life's greatest dilemma is having one of his wife Lynne's shows premiering on Broadway the same night as a midseason Red Sox game. I say *mid-season* because if it were a playoff game, there would be no issue: he would stay home to watch the Sox.

When the Red Sox fell behind 3–0 in the 2004 ALCS, Shechtman completely resigned himself to another lost year in Red

Sox Nation. While we were up to our eyeballs in advance bookings for big-assed corporate events at Mantle's, something peculiar began to happen. All but ignoring the three-game deficit, the Red Sox—the perennial underdogs, the proverbial fall guys—began to win.

"Okay," Shechtman sagely reasoned, "we won *one* game! We'll lose tomorrow."

But the next day, when the Sox won again, it only bolstered his sense of the inevitable.

"Okay, two games. Now we *have* to lose the next one."

But loose they did not, which only stoked his fury.

"Three in a row—who cares? We'll lose in game 7, on a fucking Aaron Boone home run, just like last year."

Apparently, the fact that the Yankees had canned Boone in favor of A-Rod had no bearing here. When it came to rooting for the old home team, Shechtman had grown so inured to failure that nothing could penetrate the thorny shell of his pessimism. He'd gone into this thing prepared to lose, and dammit, he was going to *lose*.

All of us Yankee fans had to agree with him. Our confidence was as deeply rooted as his doubt. As the losses mounted, we reminded each other again and again that no team in baseball history had ever come back from a 3–0 deficit to win the series.

For game 7, I rounded up my posse and watched from a table near the bar at Mickey's. There was me, Marty Appel, and my best buddies Harry Spiro and Harvey Marshak. A Cleveland native, Spiro feels the same way about The Tribe as Shechtman feels about the Sox. Spiro once ducked out of his father's funeral service to watch an Indian World Series game.

So there we were, three Yankee fans and a Yankee-hating Indian fan along for the ride. We began by sipping adult beverages, but by the time Johnny fucking Damon went yard with the sacks drunk with Red Sox, we had gone from sipping to pounding, then from pounding to chugging. I chugged to escape the reality. A Yankee loss would cost us at least $25,000 a night in additional revenue for a seven-game World Series. There would be no Christmas in October after all.

Damon's blast transformed my restaurant into a ghost town. As we say in the trade, "You could have fired a machine gun in here and not hit anyone."

As the Red Sox continued to run around the bases, my wheels began to turn.

"You know what . . ." I said to Marty. "We should hang a big sign in the window reading WELCOME TO RED SOX NATION. Or better yet," I yammered, "why don't we just change the name of the place to Ted Williams Restaurant for the Series?"

"You're a sick man, you know that?" Marty didn't like the idea at first, but he agreed to sleep on it. After sleeping on it, he decided we should go for it.

But to backtrack for a moment, there's a certain true story about Mickey that I planted in Marty's brain as we staggered out of the restaurant.

It was the 1990 Super Bowl, featuring Elway and the Broncos against Montana and the 49ers. A news crew popped into Mantle's to get the Mick's take on the big game. He answered breezily, "If the Denver Broncos don't beat the 49ers, I'll change the name of this restaurant to Joe Montana's." Then he gestured to me and stipulated, "and old Bill here will come to work in a dress."

This was the first I had heard of Mickey's love of the fish, and for the Broncos, it was the kiss of death. Mickey was the world's worst gambler. In the years when there were only thirteen college bowl games, he had gone 0–13 against the spread. Not an easy thing to do.

The Niners trounced the Broncos 55–10. Luckily, I couldn't find a dress in a size eighteen, and Mickey never did get around to renaming the place. But you get the point. As I tried later in vain to explain to Merlyn Mantle, changing the restaurant's name was essentially Mickey's idea.

Early on the morning after the greatest defeat in baseball history, Team Liederman-Appel went to work. Marty, after all, was the very first PR director for George Steinbrenner. He'd skillfully handled the controversial rebuilding of Yankee Stadium, along with the death of Thurman Munson.

We decided that I would make the signs while he hammered out a rough draft of the press release. I'm computer illiterate, so I enlisted my wife. Using her home PC, she reluctantly yet dutifully printed Ted Williams's name on two fifteen-foot sheets of banner paper. I then Velcroed these makeshift placards to the restaurant's awning, and a national controversy was born.

It was almost poetic how you could still see Mickey Mantle's logo scrawled beneath our flimsy, makeshift sign. On a clear day, you could make it out from as far as the Plaza, on the corner of Fifth Avenue, to the New York Athletic Club on the corner of Seventh. If I was *actually* going to rename my business, I think I'd at least spring for a new awning.

Everyone got our joke except the most rabid Yankee fans and the Mantle family.

When I came off the ladder after I'd finished slapping the fake sign over the real sign, Marty and I stood beneath it to admire our handiwork. We weren't alone. A crowd was already forming in front of the new "Ted Williams's Restaurant."

Early the next day, I called a punch-drunk Shechtman for some legal advice. I thought I could count on him to talk me out of it, like many of my other harebrained schemes. But Red Sox Revelry had fractured this barrister's judgment. He advised me that this was the best promotion I'd ever done and it was legally kosher. His office was only a few blocks away, and I asked him to stop by and check it out before we made it official. He arrived the next morning with a vintage Red Sox cap atop his silvery locks and a handsome face freckled with glee.

Marty's press release read as follows:

MICKEY MANTLE'S RESTAURANT IS THE TED WILLIAMS RESTAURANT FROM NOW THROUGH THE WORLD SERIES

CENTRAL PARK SOUTH LANDMARK CALLS IT A GESTURE IN THE SPIRIT OF MICKEY

New York, October 21, 2004—Mickey Mantle's Restaurant, the Central Park South fixture for more than 17 years, has posted signs over its familiar blue awning designating it as "Ted Williams Restaurant" from now through the World Series.

"The Yankees suffered this horrendous loss on what would have been Mickey's 73rd birthday," noted founder and proprietor Bill Liederman. "Mickey would have been very emotional over this— he cried when the Yankees lost to Pittsburgh on Bill Mazeroski's home run in 1960. His spirit came to me when the game was over and said, 'Bill, let's do this for my favorite player. Let's put Ted's name up there for a week.'

"Mickey would have done it from the heart, and it would have been a typically classy gesture. He enjoyed the rivalry but respected the Red Sox, and he certainly would have tipped his cap to what they just pulled off, one of the greatest stories in sports history."

The restaurant, at 42 Central Park South, was packed with fans last night, most of whom were New Yorkers stunned by what they were seeing. But there were Boston fans there as well, who celebrated the Red Sox first World Series appearance in 18 years, and perhaps, the end of the legendary "curse."

Since the Series was slated to start on a Saturday and the Yankee collapse took place on a Wednesday night, Thursday and Friday were slow news days for sports. Normally, the papers would be stuffed with the usual fluffy World Series poop and scoops: matchups, celebrity picks, inspirational stories about players who have overcome life-threatening obstacles.

Now the stories shifted from the Series to the Ted Williams Restaurant story.

The news crews began arriving in droves Thursday afternoon. The story had outgrown the sports section and was being run as a full-page story, complete with pictures, in the New York papers and all around the country. CNN ran the story on their scrolling news ticker. The phone rang nonstop, with 99 out of 100 callers calling for our heads. I couldn't expect my hostesses to put up with that abuse, so I put my daughter Chloe, Gus "the Greek," and myself in charge of fielding the calls.

The first call I answered was from a Red Sox fan, saying what a class act I was for tipping my hat to a great star like Williams, and what a good sport Yankees fans were.

My voice mail was overrun with the wrath of disgruntled Yankees fans. But two messages in particular set the tone for the entire day. The first was a stern voice mail from my landlord, who claimed I was in violation of my lease, as paper signs on his tony park-side properties are strictly forbidden. The other was a legal letter from Dorothy Weber, the Mantles' lawyer.

It turns out that someone had called Merlyn Mantle and fed her the following pieces of false information:

1. I had officially and permanently renamed the restaurant.
2. I had redecorated the restaurant all in red and white.
3. I had "forced" all my servers to don Red Sox uniforms on penalty of dismissal.

Merlyn Mantle was furious and Dorothy's missive read exactly like this:

VIA HAND DELIVERY

Mr. William Liederman
42 Central Park South
New York, NY 10019

Re: Mickey Mantle's Restaurant

Dear Mr. Liederman:

We have seen the various news reports where you advised the press that the late Mickey Mantle "came to you in a dream" and that you have covered Mickey Mantle's name with Ted Williams.

Please be advised that the Mantle family considers your conduct not only as an intentional breach of contract but also that your conduct in this regard is shameful and bizarre. This is not the first time you have shown a total lack of respect for the family but it is certainly going to be the last. Our client has instructed us to take any and all steps necessary to protect their rights. This letter shall serve as our client's notice that the agreement is hereby terminated. You are directed to cease any and all uses of the name Mickey Mantle.

Marty wanted to kill himself because he felt he had actively engaged in public relations that would result in the demise of his long-term friendship with the Mantles. For my part, I was digging the media attention until Pablo Guzmán showed up with his news crew.

Pablo Guzmán, formerly known as "Yoruba," had been a student of my father's at SUNY–Old Westbury, where he and Felipe Luciano gave birth to the "Young Lords," a militant, brown-beret-wearing, urban guerilla group calling for the complete overthrow of our government. My father even allowed them to assemble firearms in the basement playroom. Since those days, Pablo has benched the beret in favor of an Armani suit and is now a successful mainstream journalist.

"Bill," he said to me, "they just pulled me off of a murder trial in Brooklyn to come here." He then informed me that Mrs. Mantle, along with sons Danny and David, had completed a coast-to-coast telephone press hookup to denounce my actions. Their statements are best expressed by the following press release:

October 22, 2004

FOR IMMEDIATE RELEASE

Issued on Behalf of the Family of the Late
Mickey Mantle

The family of the late Mickey Mantle is shocked and outraged by Bill Liederman's conduct covering the Mickey Mantle name at Mickey Mantle's restaurant and replacing it with "Ted Williams."

"Mickey loved Ted and we hold Ted's memory in the highest regard," said Merlyn Mantle, "but Mr. Liederman's conduct is disgraceful and an insult to Mickey's memory and to the Yankees and their fans."

Danny and David Mantle went on to say, "We want everyone to know that Bill Liederman did this without the approval or knowledge of our family."

What Merlyn forgot to say was that (along with Stan Musial) Ted Williams was Mickey's baseball hero, and he would have been flattered by the association. When we talk about Ted Williams, we're talking about a man who took a five-year military leave from baseball at the prime of his career to fight for his country in World War II and Korea.

By the time darkness fell that evening, I had given interviews to over fifty reporters, which is far more than I did the day that Mickey passed. At one point, a pedicab driver burst into Mickey's screaming bloody murder: "FUCK YOU. YOU PAID MICKEY MANTLE ONE HUNDRED THOUSAND DOLLARS A YEAR TO

DRINK HIMSELF TO DEATH IN THIS BAR. BURN IN HELL, MOTHERFUCKERS! LONG LIVE THE NEW YORK YANKEES!"

After taking far too much abuse, my daughter was in the office with her head down on her desk, sobbing. Gus the Greek was MIA, having repaired to the Oak Bar, where the folks were friendly and the booze flowed for free. When he came back to work two hours later, the battle was still raging.

Bending under the pressure supplied by my landlord, the Mantles, and the angry mob, I took the sign down. This did little or nothing to ease the media crush. I remained in the restaurant, giving interviews and issuing statements until the following voice mail forced me to fold up my tent: "You're dead. Your kids are dead. We know where you live. Your days on this earth are numbered, you money-grubbing Jew bastard."

On my way out the door, I was treated to a live TV interview with Merlyn Mantle and Len Berman on CBS. Merlyn called me "disrespectful," "hurtful," "horrible," "misguided," "shameful," and "sacrilegious." How had we gotten here? I had always considered Merlyn to be like family. We had celebrated together at birthdays and weddings, and cried together at funerals.

Marty and I listened to the music of the media and changed our tune. In the spirit of mea culpa, I sent a letter of apology to the Mantle family. I said I'd made a huge mistake, but the rebel in me had a different take: *We're tipping our hats to the miracle Red Sox,* I thought. *Mickey would have wanted it that way. It's a shout-out to Steinbrenner who, despite his payroll budget of over 200 million dollars a year, suffered the most stupendous collapse in baseball history. Bring back Tino! Bring back Brosius! Bring back O'Neill!*

When all was said and done, the sports world was talking not about the Sox versus Cardinals World Series, but about the all-time Series hero, Mickey Mantle. For forty-eight hours, it was all Mickey, all the time. The man with ten World Series titles and a record-breaking eighteen Series home runs had just enjoyed a second wave of celebrity from beyond the grave.

I took a bunch of calls from wacky drive-time DJs in various cities such as Boston, Chicago, and Los Angeles. "On the phone, live from New York, is Bill Liederman," one DJ declared, "the man who *sold out* the Yankees! Bill, can you explain your *out-raaageous* behavior?"

As Friday drew to a close, Mike the Cop stopped by to suggest that I get out of town for forty-eight hours, so I packed my family into a rented SUV on Saturday morning and made fast tracks for our country cottage in the backwoods of eastern Pennsylvania.

Merlyn caught me on the phone as I was zipping up my weekend bag, getting ready to leave. I had been screamed at by women before (including women I had cheated on), but nothing compared with the acid shrieks of Mrs. Mantle. This devoutly religious woman was swearing at me like a longshoreman with a red-hot poker up his ass.

She told me the Mantle family wanted nothing to do with me. She also demanded that I take Mickey's name off the restaurant for good.

I played rope-a-dope for a minute or two, until her voice began to turn hoarse, then calmed down.

"Merlyn, I'm sorry. It was just a practical joke, the type Mickey used to enjoy."

She wasn't having any of it.

"This isn't April-effing-Fools' Day, you idiot!"

"Look, I know you feel strongly about this," I reasoned, "but I'm raising four kids on this restaurant. This is my livelihood. Furthermore," I ventured, "the restaurant has furnished the Mantle family with over a million dollars in licensing fees alone."

"The money you paid our family is a *pittance*," she hissed, "a *pittance*, do you hear me?"

There was nothing left to say, so we bade each other a bristly farewell. Merlyn's phone call had spent most of her venom, and the ice was beginning to thaw.

The Liederman clan left town, and once we reached the West Side Highway, I popped on the radio, scanning the dial to find any station covering the story. They all were. WFAN, ESPN, WINS, and WCBS were harping on a single topic: the Ted Williams Restaurant. A movie fugitive would have shut off the radio (or ripped it out of the dashboard), but I hunkered down and took in every word. For the next forty minutes, I listened—so intently that I didn't even hear the are-we-there-yet cries from the backseat.

I was called a mercenary and a traitor by Curtis Silva, the famed Guardian Angel with the red jacket and red beret. "He must be out if his *mind*," Silva marveled, his hatred for the Sox spewing out over the airwaves.

In all my years of listening to sports radio, I had never called into a station to say, "Hello, this is Bill from Manhattan. *First-time caller, longtime listener.*"

My cell phone was dead, so I had to pull off the road at a Sunoco station and find a pay phone from which to dial the *Curtis & Kirby Show.* The switchboard wasted no time putting me through to Curtis, who immediately put my call on the air and proceeded to go postal.

"Hey, Curtis," I queried, "did you see *The New York Times* today?

There was a photo of Governor Pataki on the front page of the Metro section. He wore a Red Sox uniform to work at the State House."

"So?" Curtis probed.

"So leave me alone. I put up a transparent paper sign! If I had worn a Red Sox jersey like the governor did, we wouldn't be having this conversation because I'd be lying in a ditch somewhere."

He had to agree with that, and he cut me off.

When we arrived at our country house, I got a call from Don Patrick on ESPN Radio. While a national audience listened, Patrick began by sarcastically/indignantly reading the press release that the Mantles had issued the day before. I was eager to respond, but he gonged me before I could defend myself.

The next call was from the NYPD, informing me that, due to numerous bomb threats, several patrol cars would remain parked outside the restaurant for the rest of the weekend.

The time in the country did right by me, and by Monday morning, The Ted Williams Hoax had faded into yesterday's news. My fifteen minutes of fame had all but elapsed.

Two weeks later, I got a call from Danny Mantle, by far the most sensitive and articulate of the Mantle boys. With nervous laughter, we began to rehash Ted-gate. At the end of our strained conversation, he said to me, "Yo, man . . . it probably all would have been okay if you hadn't covered up mah ol' daddy's name. It just ain't right to do that to mah daddy. Know what ah mean, Billy?"

I thought of my own father and stepfather, who had both passed on during that baseball season, and at that moment, I understood.

"You're right," I told him. "I know exactly what you mean." And suddenly, miraculously, there was peace in the valley.

Upstairs, the restaurant was teeming with curious customers. Bad press, my ass: the bad press was packing the joint. Marty had to agree, but with one critical exception.

"You know what I learned from this?" he asked me.

"To find a better brand of client," I guessed.

"No—that whatever you do in this town, you never tread on the sacred ground of Yankee lore. It just isn't done."

28

TUNA MELTDOWN

As Dr. Ed Brown attached the last electrode to my finger and instructed me to stare at the wall, I could feel the sweat beading up on my temples. Wires hung from my arms and chest in thick garlands as Doc Brown switched on the polygraph machine and pulled out a list of questions.

"Are the lights on in this room?" he asked me.

"Yes," I replied. There was little activity from the wire claw as it scratched its way across the paper.

"Is your name Bill Liederman?"

"Yes."

"Have you ever lied to anyone who loved or trusted you?"

Hel-lo! That'll wake you up in the morning. Before I could answer, a series of questions tore through my mind. *What is love? What is trust?* But who was I kidding? Like every kid, I had lied to my parents, and I had lied to various women. Now I lied on the lie detector test, hoping that I could out-think the lie detector machine.

No sooner had the lie escaped my lips than the needle began to swerve wildly about, as if in protest. In fact, the entire machine seemed to percolate with indignation. I saw the doc make a mark on his list before stampeding on to the next question.

"Have you ever broken the law and gotten away with it?"

Who hasn't? I thought, as visions of recreational drugs, junior high shoplifting, speeding, and those extra three frames at the bowling alley danced in my head.

"No," I lied, and the needle scarred the page with inky zigzags. I winced.

The next question pertained more closely to the matter at hand: "Did you leave the Ben Ash deli without paying for your wife's tuna melt?"

"Yes," I answered, and the needle bobbed peacefully along in agreement.

"Did you leave the Ben Ash deli without paying the check?"

"No," I answered. "I paid for everything but the tuna melt."

"Just yes or no, please," the doc cut in. Again, "Did you pay for everything else except your wife's tuna melt?"

"Yes," I said triumphantly, as the needle seconded that emotion.

I'd been truthful about the tuna sandwich, and soon, a national TV audience would know it.

After shutting down the machine and disentangling the mess of wires, Dr. Brown said it was time for my interview with *Lie Detector* host Rolanda Watts. After that, we'd shoot a reenactment of the test, followed by a "reveal." They'd offered me a $2,000 appearance fee, plus airfare, room, and board. I could smell my own fear as Dr. Brown sent me packing for my rendezvous with Rolanda Watts.

"Can't you just tell me how I did?" I asked on my way out his office. "Thumbs up or thumbs down?"

"You have to wait until the reveal," the doc responded, with all the bedside manner of Dr. Kevorkian.

I looked back to December 29, the height of the holiday season in the Big Apple, and I was gifted four front-row tickets to the Big Apple Circus. My wife and I left our brand-new baby, Theodora, with my oldest daughter, Chloe, and herded the other two kids off to the big top temporarily residing at Lincoln Center.

After the show, we hit the street in search of a bite to eat. Our first two choices, Brooklyn Diner and the Carnegie Deli, had lines around the block estimated at a wait of over an hour and a half. In restaurant patois, anything over an hour wait means "get lost." As a rule of thumb, an estimated wait time of forty-five minutes or less means, "Stick around, you won't regret it. I'll probably be able to seat you earlier." Any idiot who actually waits over an hour to be seated can expect to wait another hour for the beleaguered kitchen to dig their way out of hell and actually serve the food. By the time you have paid the tab, you'll have spent almost three hours in the restaurant, which is a total waste of time, considering you still have to get to the Statue of Liberty, the Empire State Building, Ground Zero, the Build-a-Bear Workshop, and the American Girl place.

We moved on. The next place we happened upon was Ben Ash delicatessen. A second-rate pile of bricks that fed off of impatient queue-standers at Carnegie Deli directly across the street, the sign outside of Ben Ash trumpeted: WHY WAIT IN LINE WHEN YOU CAN EAT HERE, NOW?

Here's why. Once we'd been seated at Ben Ash, my daughter ordered spaghetti and meatballs, and my son chose pizza. Without hesitating, our waiter vetoed the order.

"I really wouldn't order that," he warned. "Believe me, the kids won't touch the food."

A ringing endorsement, if I ever heard one.

We changed our order to chicken fingers and fries for the kids, pastrami for me, and a tuna melt for my wife, even though I had tried to explain to her on many occasions that you just don't order a tuna melt in a Jewish delicatessen.

"Tuna melt . . . Oh-kaaay," the waiter said, eyeing us as if to say, "Stay away."

His response didn't inspire a whole lot of confidence, but at this point we pretty much wanted to eat, pay, and get the hell out.

The food arrived almost *too* quickly, and our waiter asked us if the food was okay as he was placing the entrees on the table. It was a weird question, because nobody had tasted any of the food yet.

I inhaled my pastrami sandwich in four and a half bites while my wife played Mother Hen, cutting the children's chicken fingers and dropping large blobs of ketchup on their plates. By the time she actually tasted her tuna melt, we were already fifteen minutes into the meal.

She took one bite, spit it right back out into her napkin, and let out a little yelp. "Ogggh," she choked, "that's nasty! It tastes like cat food."

Curious, and still hungry, I followed suit—with the very same result.

"You're right; that *is* nasty," I agreed, peeling back the English muffin to reveal two dark brown lumps of pasty fish covered with a blob of Cheez Whiz.

I flagged down the waiter and handed him the virtually untouched plate of food.

"What can I bring you instead?" he asked.

"Nothing, thanks. Just take it off the check and that'll be all."

"I'm afraid the management has a no-backsies policy . . . Once the waiter serves the food, you *own* it. When I brought the food, I asked you if everything was okay, and you said yes."

"We hadn't tasted the food yet," I explained.

"Then you should have *said* you hadn't tasted it yet. You should *not* have said everything was okay."

I was truly astonished. I'd been in the restaurant business for a quarter of a century and I never once refused to take off the check something that didn't taste good. The policy at Mantle's was so liberal that, even if a customer had eaten almost all of it, we'd take it off the check if he wasn't satisfied. The restaurant business is about making friends, not enemies. Bad word of mouth is the death knell for any eatery, so at Mantle's, the customer was *always* king—even if he acted like King Kong.

"So you're not gonna take it off the check?" I asked in disbelief.

"I can't," he replied simply. "I don't make the rules."

"Then let me speak to someone who does," I said, getting to my feet. I wanted to hear the manager say we had to pay for that rancid fish.

An Israeli man about half my size met me in the middle of the packed dining room, stuck his index finger in my face, and proceeded to lecture me about the "no-backsies" policy.

"That's swell, but I'm just *not* paying for skanky fish. Here's $46 dollars for everything else, plus tax and tip. Good-bye."

Before I could get back to the table to help the kids put on their coats, he began screaming at me.

"You don't pay for that tuna melt, I call police," he hollered. "You go to jail, like *thief*!"

"Hey, chief, you can call the National Guard for all I care. Kids, let's go."

As we stepped into the weather vestibule, a tag team of Ben Ash staffers burst into what looked like a well-rehearsed drill designed to hold customers hostage. A group of six amigos were now fully deployed to prevent our immediate departure. Four of them barricaded the door from the outside, while the rest of the retention team leaned against the inside door, trapping us inside four glass walls. Clearly, I wasn't the first person who'd refused to pay for a rancid sandwich.

By this time, four-year-old Emmy had started to wail. My wife started beating on the door with clenched fists. The busboys pushed back at her so hard that she fell backward into a potted plant, tripping over Emmy in the process. My adrenaline flowed as I pondered my three options: I could make like Buford Pusser by grabbing a bar stool and busting up the place; I could wait for the police; or I could bust out with my family immediately. I went with option three.

With escape the plan, I gathered the wife and kids protectively in my arms and morphed into a human battering ram. I knocked the busboys over like bowling pins and burst out onto the street with my brood in tow.

Emmy was still crying. "Daddy," she sobbed, "people are supposed to use helping hands, not hurting hands!"

My six-year-old son, Mack, always the wise guy, weighed in with, "Well, I guess we won't be eating there again, will we, Dad?"

I'm sure the kids were wondering how a nice afternoon at the circus could end up in a brawl. I fell asleep that night kicking myself for not kicking the shit out of everyone at Ben Ash.

The next day I repeated the story to my publicist. I thought it might make an interesting one-liner for one of the local gossip columns, kind of a restaurant-versus-restaurant thing. Within the hour, the *New York Daily News* dispatched a reporter and photographer to Mantle's.

The next day's paper had wall-to-wall tsunami coverage, but for some reason, the editors at the *Daily News* decided to run our tale of tuna terror as an exclusive feature splashed over almost all of page 20. In the midst of the tsunami stories, the headline blared, "Fish Story Turned Ugly at Midtown Deli Tuna Melt-Down." The article that followed was fairly accurate, with the exception of the unnamed owner's comments. "Liederman didn't pay *any* of the bill," he claimed. "He threatened the waiter and even punched a manager in the face. If he tries to sue us, we'll destroy him."

According to him, I had planned all along to beat the check at Ben Ash.

Over the course of the next month, several people approached me in the neighborhood. "Hey," they'd say, "aren't you that tuna melt guy?" It turned out all of them had had eerily similar experiences at Ben Ash, right down to the rotten tuna melt. They'd all been browbeaten into paying for it anyway, and they admired my refusal to cooperate with this Israeli idiot.

I received a phone call from the producers of *Lie Detector,* a reality show that used a polygraph machine to determine if guests were guilty or innocent.

The host was Rolanda Watts, who had once been one of my favorite New York news anchors. The producers thought the tuna melt snafu would make a fun episode, complete with food puns and all the general silliness of my scenario. Other far more serious guests on the show had included Paula Jones and the Ramseys.

I agreed to appear on the show, and two weeks later I was sitting in an LA greenroom, waiting to begin my sequel. Waiting with me was a silent, brooding woman whose situation made mine seem to be even more trivial.

The question she was about to be asked on TV was: Did the one-pound bag of cocaine that your husband gave you when the LAPD broke down your door, the bag that you subsequently tried to swallow, in fact belong to you?

She explained on the air that her ex-husband had a long rap sheet, and the cops were almost certain that it was his stash—in fact, given his priors, they indicted him and made him a guest of the state until his 120th birthday. She was trying to spring him by copping to possession. Because she had no priors, she figured she'd get off with probation, and her husband would walk. It was a sad act to follow.

As I walked into the studio for my reveal, I could almost hear Rolanda announcing: *He may not have punched the manager but he had lied to the people who loved and trusted him, and he has broken the law and gotten away with it . . .* I'd lied about love, trust, and everything that mattered, but I'd come squeaky clean with regard to a stinking sandwich. I'd already signed a waiver, so short of fleeing the studio, I was all in.

Rolanda Watts asked me why I had come all the way out to LA to appear on the show. In response, I took the Eddie Haskell route: "On behalf of all my fellow restaurateurs, I want to assure the people of New York, as well as visitors from around the globe, that the behavior of the Ben Ash deli staff is indeed an aberration, and that most restaurant owners actually *want* repeat business . . . I just couldn't let one bad apple spoil the Big Apple."

The truth wouldn't have played out as well: I am a publicity hound; plus, they offered me $2,000 and a free trip to LA.

When it was time for my reveal, the director brought me back out on stage with Rolanda. She welcomed us back from the break.

"Bill Liederman," she began, "you have come all the way from New York City to set the record straight and prove to the entire nation that you were truthful about your tuna melt. Are you ready to learn the results of your lie detector test?"

I nodded.

Ro pinched the envelope, brandished it seductively, and slit it open with her long, mauve fingernails.

"Bill Liederman," she said, and after a ten-second pause: "You told . . . the truth!"

I could feel the voice of Marv Albert rising inside of me, saying *YES!*

"Is there anything else you want to say here today?" Rolanda asked, peering at me from beneath her thick, batting eyelashes.

"Yeah," I said, "you look beautiful."

29

LAST CALL

THIS IS WHERE the shit really hits the fan.

I had been forced to declare bankruptcy as a result of the Nyack catastrophe and had to relinquish my ownership share of Mantle's to the bankruptcy trustee. A business associate bought up all of my interests, as well as the interests of all the other partners. The new owner brought in his son and the son's best friend to oversee the operation. At some point, the three of them decided that my highly compensated services were no longer necessary, and they sent me a letter terminating my services.

The day after my beheading, I went into Mantle's at 6:00 a.m. to collect my personal belongings. The next day, Mike the Cop informed me that there was a bench warrant out for my arrest for breaking and entering and grand larceny theft. He advised me to report to the Midtown North precinct, ASAP.

Chloe came to provide moral support. When we got to the station house, a detective led us into his office to tell me I was under arrest for theft of several pictures from Mantle's.

"Okay, wait," I interjected, "I went into the restaurant through an open door and picked up my personal effects, as per the owner's instructions."

"What kind of personal effects?" the detective pressed.

"Some pictures of my daughter, a picture of myself on the cover of a Wheaties box, and a couple of autographed pictures made out to me from Mickey."

"Well, he doesn't know what you took, but he says he's sure you took certain items that belong to the restaurant."

"Tell him that if you let me go now, I will have the pictures back in his hands by midnight tonight, even though they don't belong to him."

"It's too late for that," he insisted. "We're going to have to keep you overnight. Since it's late in the day, we may have to transfer you downtown to the Tombs for processing. But because you have some good friends in the department, we will try to keep you here in our luxury suites for the night." I quickly accepted my fate, and the luxury suite sounded pretty good to me.

I guess I should have asked to see a lawyer, but at this point I wasn't thinking clearly and figured that after a good night's sleep, I could sort everything out in the morning. The detective assured me that if this collar was wrong, I could take legal action against the plaintiff for false imprisonment. That lifted my spirits measurably.

My daughter gave me a bear hug before they hauled me off to my suite, situated right across from Detective Row. Once inside, I discovered that the suite was actually a standard issue prison-movie jail cell. I had four cellmates, including a Middle Eastern man who had fallen asleep on the floor with a bag of pita bread on his chest and a teenage boy in a tutu, rocking back and forth on the hard wooden bench like Leo Mazzone, the pitching coach for the Baltimore Orioles.

Soon those two were hauled off, leaving me alone with the other two guys. One of them, a short and muscle-bound man in a suit, paced back and forth in the cell like a tropical fish on amphetamines, bouncing off the sides of the tank. I put on my social worker cap and tried to calm him down.

He was a graduate of Notre Dame and was working as an investment banker for Smith Barney. He lived in Morristown, New Jersey, with his wife and three kids—ages six, eight, and ten. Several months earlier, his wife had discovered that he was having an affair with "another married person with children," someone he worked with who also lived in Morristown. For almost three years, the two of them conducted a spectacular and secretive affair. The two families traveled together, did the Club Med thing, and enjoyed countless backyard barbeques in each other's company. Their children even played on the same Little League teams.

As he told his sorry story, I noticed that he was having trouble with his pronouns. At first he referred to his lover as "this particular individual," then he switched to "she." Then he slipped up by referring to his lover as a "he" and finally threw his hands up in the air, as if he were surrendering.

"Who am I trying to kid?" he asked himself. "I had an affair with a man. I'm gay. I'm fucking gay!"

I asked him if he had always been gay.

"No," he said, "I never thought I was, but when I met this man at work, I fell head over heels in love with him. We traveled together and worked together all day long."

"Was *he* always gay?" I asked.

"He used to live in the Village, where he had a very active gay lifestyle. Then he went deep into the closet and came out married."

He told me that his lover had dumped him for another guy

after abusing him physically by slapping his face in the car and curs-ing him out. He said over and over again that all he wanted was an apology. It sounded to me that what he really wanted was his boyfriend back.

The talking seemed to calm him down, and he stopped his pac-ing to sit down next to me on the hard wooden bench. He asked me what I thought he should do. "The truth will set you free," I said. "When you get out of here, go home to your wife and tell her the whole truth. Maybe you'll forge a new and better relationship between the two of you."

"I can't tell her I'm gay," he protested. "What if the children find out?"

"So be it," I said. "Maybe this would be a good time to get a place of your own and see your kids on the weekends. You'll spend more quality time with your kids than you are spending now."

I asked him what I believe to be the most important question regarding the strength of a relationship: "When something good, bad, or funny happens to you, who do you tell first?"

"Up until recently, my boyfriend," he said, "but before that, my wife was the *last* person I would ever talk to about anything impor-tant. We only talk about the kids."

"Do you think this could change?"

"No," he said, "we're just too different."

I asked him what he was in jail for.

"Like I told you, all I wanted was an apology. And when I didn't get it, I wrote a letter to his wife, his kids, and some of our mutual friends. I outed the bastard."

"And yourself, in the process."

"I don't care," he burst out saying, "because I finally got my revenge on him."

"That's bullshit," I said. "He probably told everyone that you're crazy and denied everything you wrote.

"You can take this to the Smith Barney bank: first of all, you and this guy are finished forever; he's obviously moved on—and you should do the same. Holding onto this anger toward him will ruin your life."

It was then that the cops took him away, either to another suite, or downtown to the Tombs. When he left, he thanked me and said he felt much better as a result of our conversation.

Now I was alone with Jeff, a tall, burly, woodsy-looking guy who'd had a twenty-year career in environmental cleanup. On September 11, he was on the roof of a building adjacent to the Twin Towers, supervising an asbestos removal job. He watched in utter shock as the first plane plowed into the tower. He said the second plane came in low, directly over the roof he was working on. He said the bottom of the plane actually grazed the top of his head, and that he was suffering from post-traumatic stress disorder as a result of his ordeal.

Every day, he stopped in for a cup of coffee at The Coffee Pot on 49th and Ninth Avenue. He had gotten friendly with a young counter girl from Ecuador with a boyfriend who lived south of the border nine months out of the year. She talked about getting a better job, and Jeff offered to help her with her resumé. She gladly e-mailed it to him.

Jeff never saw her outside the luncheonette. He described her as being very sweet, but homely.

When the boyfriend returned from Ecuador, he read her e-mails and found the correspondence with Jeff regarding her resumé. He found Jeff's phone number and started calling him at all hours of the night, accusing him of stepping out with his woman.

Jeff's ailing father lived Upstate, and every time the phone rang at odd hours of the night, he prayed that it was not the call he had been dreading, announcing his death. Finally, one morning at 5:00 a.m., the boyfriend called again, and Jeff snapped. "Listen," he said, "if you don't stop calling me, I'm going to track you down and kill you."

In my mind, *track you down and kill you* is a figure of speech, but the boyfriend didn't feel that way. He recorded the conversation and personally delivered the tape to the station house. Jeff had been incarcerated for threatening a man's life on the phone.

I learned two lessons from these pretty good guys: don't put anything in writing, including e-mails or poison pen letters, and certainly don't leave threatening messages.

Finally, they moved me into the west wing of the precinct, but not before printing and cuffing me. The newfangled electronic fingerprint machine was not in the mood to cooperate, and I stood there for over an hour as a rookie cop tried to make the thing work. Finally, they recuffed me and took me to my cell to meet my new roommate.

He was a tall, skinny black man—heavily pierced and inked up, wearing clothes that would have fit Andre the Giant. He was in for possession of ten bags of crack while trespassing. The new suite was less than half the size of the old one. It contained one stainless steel toilet bowl with no toilet paper, and one butcher block of a bench about four feet long. Homeboy was bouncing off the walls, detoxing and howling like a wolf. After three hours of this madness, the prison matron took pity on me and switched me to a private cell on the upper tier.

Detectives love to make easy collars because a collar means extra paperwork; extra paperwork means overtime; overtime means extra money. The detectives strut up and down Detective Row chanting "ca-ching, ca-ching, ca-ching."

There's no meal plan for skells, so at dinnertime, the cops make a big deal out of opening large containers of Chinese food, pizza, and the like and chowing down with moans of pleasure right in front of us scumbags. My daughter brought me a sandwich from Carnegie Deli, which was added to their buffet.

Once I had settled down in my own private jail cell, I tried in vain to sleep, but it was too cold. I wasn't provided with a blanket, mattress, or pillow. If I put my jacket on, I had no pillow; and if I used my jacket for a pillow, it was too cold to sleep. I tried pacing. I did 1,000 sit-ups. Finally, I fell asleep for about an hour.

When I woke up, it was four in the morning. I knew that I wouldn't be in front of the judge until at least 9:00 a.m., and the time moved slower than the clock in my seventh-grade algebra class. After I thought an hour had gone by, I peeked at my watch: it had been less than five minutes.

A few minutes before nine o'clock, there was finally some human contact: a female prison guard brought me a breakfast of warm Diet Coke and a cold Egg McMuffin. I definitely *wasn't* lovin' it, and I didn't eat it.

After breakfast, I realized I could no longer boycott my stainless steel toilet. Unable to hold it, I relieved myself. Without the luxury of toilet paper. I tried the McDonald's wrapper as a shit ticket, but it was waxy and provided no traction. My only choice was to McWipe my McAss with the discarded McMuffin.

Around noon, Mike the Cop stopped by with a contraband copy of the *New York Post,* two slices of pizza, and a roll of toilet paper.

As the afternoon wore on, I started to stress out. I knew from the day before that the judge left at 4:00 p.m. sharp. If I wasn't seen by then, I would have to stay another night. Mercifully, with the court day almost over, they handcuffed me to five other skells in a daisy chain and led us into community court right next door.

I was appointed a public defender by the name of Gallo, like in *My Cousin Vinny.*

"Is it Gallo or Callow, with a C?" I joked.

"Gallo. With a G."

He didn't get it.

Once inside the courtroom, the public defenders brought the perps before the judge and after a whirlwind of activity, each case was adjudicated in under sixty seconds.

When my case came up, Gallo-with-a-G plead not guilty on my behalf. After hearing the particulars of the case, the judge dropped the charges and set me free.

After getting sprung from the pokey, two things were perfectly clear: Mantle's new owner had completed the grand coup d'état, and I was suddenly out of the restaurant business, unemployed and penniless. Despite the serious nature of my predicament, I was surprised at the sense of relief it brought me. *I'm out of the restaurant business,* I chanted out loud, over and over. It was time for me to stop bothering with busboys, uniforms, glasses, the price of hamburger meat, messy bathrooms, and daily cash crunches. It was time to stop worrying about what people ate and drank. My work at Mickey's was over. It had been a great run of EIGHTEEN YEARS!

It was time for me to start my fourth career. I was hired by Air America to do a sports talk radio show with ESPN's Larry Hardest and power-lifting Hall of Famer Nance Avigliano. Several years ago, I had started to dabble in radio, hosting radio sports talk shows. Over time, I had spun that dabbling into a second career, doing shows for WFAS in Hartsdale and a daily radio show "Live From Mantle's" on

WCTC in New Brunswick. I had learned how to host sports talk radio by watching and learning from the dozens of radio show hosts who had broadcast live from Mickey's over the years: Spencer Ross and the Amazin' (or amazin'ly full of himself) Bill Mazer; the Soul Man and the Coleman; even Don Imus, the greatest shock jock of all time. We also hosted Dandy Dan Daniels's country music show, Mark Simone of WNEW, and Michael Kay and John Sterling of WABC.

I also saw the hard side of the radio business, such as when Spencer Ross was fired at the broadcasting table immediately after his show, in front of friends and family, by the ruthless general manager, Mark Mason. Spencer was about to go off on a week's vacation and the station had told him that Mazer would fill in for him. Right after his show was over, WFAN listeners listened to the introduction of Bill Mazer as the permanent replacement for Spencer's spot. Spencer and I had become fast friends, even buying a trotter named Big Walt together, who didn't start winning until we sold him. I was disappointed he was fired.

After Bill was dumped in favor of Ed Coleman and Dave Simms, I hadn't heard from him for a year, when he called me at Mantle's to ask me if I could hook him up with a freebie limo for the evening. I asked him why he was calling me now. He said, "I didn't need you until now!"

A week or so after I was sprung from the pokey, I walked to Mantle's to say hello/goodbye to some of my employees, some of whom had been with me for fifteen years. When I arrived, I noticed a fat busboy with jiggling man breasts wearing an ill-fitting Mickey Mantle's jersey half-tucked into a pair of wrinkled trousers. A cell phone was clipped to his belt, and a filthy kitchen towel was draped over his shoulder. As he leaned over to bus tables, the dirty rag dangled in the customers' faces. Unable to resist the temptation, I waved Gus the Greek over, just for old time's sake.

"Gus," I said, "I know it's not my business, but that busboy . . ."

"I know," he answered. "I'll get right on that, Mr. Liederman."

I laughed. That was what he always said, directly prior to doing absolutely nothing.

Our Saturday morning radio show on Air America, "The Sporting Blues," soon doubled its ratings and our ratings topped ESPN's Saturday morning programming. After six months, we were let go in favor of paid programming by the cash-starved Air America.

After spending the balance of the year trying in vain to invent a new non-food business, I begrudgingly returned to the business I know best.

I didn't want to open another sports place, and after months of agonizing contemplation, I finally conjured up a restaurant called Burgers and Cupcakes located in the old Krispy Kreme location on West 23rd Street in the city, marked by a giant, illuminated revolving pink cupcake on top of the canopy. We service fifteen flavors of all-butter cupcakes and nine types of burgers from turkey to ostrich and that's all! I am often asked, "Why burgers and cupcakes?"

"Why?" I reply. "Because people love them!"